THE
ARMED FORCES
OFFICER

THE
ARMED FORCES
OFFICER

U.S. Department of Defense

NATIONAL DEFENSE UNIVERSITY PRESS
WASHINGTON, D.C.

POTOMAC BOOKS, INC.
WASHINGTON, D.C.

Co-published in the United States by National Defense University Press and Potomac Books, Inc. The opinions, conclusions, and recommendations expressed or implied within are those of the authors and do not necessarily reflect the views of the Department of Defense or any other agency of the Federal Government. This publication is cleared for public release; distribution unlimited. Portions of this book may be quoted or reprinted without further permission, with credit to both National Defense University Press and Potomac Books, Inc.

Library of Congress Cataloging-in-Publication Data

Hardcover ISBN-13: 978-1-59797-166-9

Softcover ISBN-13: 978-1-59797-167-6

(alk. paper)

Printed in the United States of America on acid-free paper that meets the American National Standards Institute Z39-48 Standard.

Available from:

Potomac Books, Inc.
22841 Quicksilver Drive
Dulles, Virginia 20166
800-775-2518

2007 Edition

10 9 8 7 6 5 4 3 2

Upon being commissioned in the Armed Services of the United States, a man incurs a lasting obligation to cherish and protect his country and to develop within himself that capacity and reserve strength which will enable him to serve its arms and the welfare of his fellow Americans with increasing wisdom, diligence, and patriotic conviction.

This is the meaning of the commission.

S. L. A. Marshall

Requirement of Exemplary Conduct

Title 10 US Code, Section 5947:

All commanding officers and others in authority in the naval service are required to show in themselves a good example of virtue, honor, patriotism, and subordination; to be vigilant in inspecting the conduct of all persons who are placed under their command; to guard against and suppress all dissolute and immoral practices, and to correct, according to the laws and regulations of the Navy, all persons who are guilty of them; and to take all necessary and proper measures, under the laws, regulations and customs of the naval service, to promote and safeguard the morale, the physical well-being, and the general welfare of the officers and enlisted persons under their command or charge.

Title 10 US Code, Sections 3583, 85831:

All commanding officers and others in authority in the Army/Air Force are required—

(1) to show in themselves a good example of virtue, honor, patriotism, and subordination;

(2) to be vigilant in inspecting the conduct of all persons who are placed under their command;

(3) to guard against and suppress all dissolute and immoral practices, and to correct, according to the laws and regulations of the Army/Air Force, all persons who are guilty of them; and

(4) to take all necessary and proper measures, under the laws, regulations and customs of the Army/Air Force, to promote and safeguard the morale, the physical well-being, and the general welfare of the officers and enlisted persons under their command or charge.

CONTENTS

FOREWORD

GENERAL PETER PACE
UNITED STATES MARINE CORPS
CHAIRMAN OF THE JOINT CHIEFS OF STAFF

General George C. Marshall, Chief of Staff of the Army and later Secretary of Defense, said during World War II, "We are determined that before the sun sets on this terrible struggle, our flag will be recognized throughout the world as a symbol of freedom on the one hand and overwhelming force on the other." The Nation was at war in Europe and Japan, and although the struggle was very different from the one in which we are currently engaged, the themes that define our profession of arms and guide the actions of our officers apply today just as they did over 60 years ago.

The uncertainties of today's world and the nature of our adversaries increase the importance of these ideas. They provide a foundation upon which you should build as you prepare to meet tomorrow's objectives. The time and effort spent developing this groundwork will pay dividends as you confront new and unique challenges in the years ahead.

I encourage you to reflect on the timeless themes outlined in this book and consider what honor, integrity, selflessness, commitment, and the greater good mean to you. They define the ethos of our profession of arms, a philosophy that has moral leadership at its core. Vice Admiral James Stockdale, Vietnam POW and Medal of Honor recipient, once said, "... even in the most detached duty, we warriors must keep foremost in our minds that there are boundaries to the prerogatives of leadership, moral boundaries." As you read these pages and think about their meaning, do so expecting to be called upon to apply moral leadership in situations where your life, the lives of your troops, and the safety and security of the United States hang in the balance.

Your commission and oath of office are reminders of your higher calling to our great Nation and Constitution. As you embark on your military career, I ask you to dedicate your study to the men and women you will one day have the privilege to lead and command.

PETER PACE
General, United States Marine Corps
Chairman of the Joint Chiefs of Staff

FOREWORD

THE HONORABLE IKE SKELTON (D–MO)

I am continually impressed with the members of the Armed Forces, impressed and grateful for all they do. The same goes for their families who endure long months of separation and danger of loss. Each time I think we can ask no more of them, they find another way to surprise me. Their resilience is amazing, and the nation is grateful.

This new edition, written while the nation is at war, is a successor to a classic series written the first time in 1950 by journalist-historian S. L. A. Marshall at the behest of General George C. Marshall, America's greatest soldier-statesman of the last century. George Marshall never led troops in battle, but he spent much of his long and distinguished military career educating and training officers for war. He formed the great citizen-army that won the global mid-century wars against Nazi tyranny and Japanese imperial designs. George Marshall was a pioneer of service unity, what we call "jointness," and unity of command in operational forces. S. L. A. Marshall, explaining the purpose of his book, attributed it to Marshall's belief that officers of all services founded their professional commitment on a common moral-ethical grounding, a grounding the author of that first volume set out to explain.

This new edition takes up George Marshall's inspirational premise and S. L. A. Marshall's example and carries them into the new century. The book aims to educate commissioned officers of all services, as well as interested outsiders, about the basic moral-ethical requirements of being a commissioned officer in the Armed Forces of the United States. Understanding the common foundation of commissioned leadership and command of American military forces is essential if we are to achieve true excellence in joint operations; it unites the officers of the separate services in a common calling of supporting, defending, and bearing true faith and allegiance to the Constitution, and in providing good and faithful service in performance of the military officer's duty.

The book begins by emphasizing the officer's oath and commission, observing the implications of the Constitutional division of military authority between the state and federal governments and of constitutional authority and responsibility for civil control of federal forces between the legislative, executive, and judicial branches. These divisions are sometimes difficult to negotiate, but they are the foundation of American liberty. The nation is ill served when the leadership of the armed forces is inadequately attentive to the different roles and responsibilities of the separate branches. The nation is stronger when the American people fully understand them and demand their respect.

This book is intended to be the first volume in the professional library of newly commissioned officers, the first brick in a lifetime of professional military education, supported by institutional periods of quality collective instruction and inquiry, expanded by progressive operational experience, but ultimately shaped by habitual individual study and reflection throughout the military career. Broad continuous education—technical, conceptual, and moral-ethical—is the hallmark of a professional officer. The armed forces officer's career must be designed to encourage and support a lifetime quest for knowledge and understanding of all aspects of the officer's vocation.

The American armed forces are amazing institutions. I have watched them at peace and war longer than most men and women in uniform. These brave and creative Americans have never failed to meet the challenges set before them and they have more than a few facing them today. The indomitable spirit of the thousands of wounded men and women, regulars and reservists, fighting to remain on active duty in spite of their wounds, is ample evidence of the well-being of the institutional soul of today's armed forces, its men and women of all ranks. It is into the hands of armed forces officers that the leadership of these men and women is entrusted by the American people, through their elected representatives and government. This book is a modest effort to explain the nature of that trust and the obligations and expectations it entails.

CONGRESSMAN IKE SKELTON (D–MO)
Ranking Member, House Armed Services Committee

INTRODUCTION

THE MEANING OF THE COMMISSION

As an officer in the Armed Forces of the United States you are a citizen-soldier, a warrior in the profession of arms, a member of a skilled profession, an unwavering defender of the Constitution and a servant of the nation. A leader of character, you accept unmitigated personal responsibility and accountability to duty, for your actions and those of your subordinates. You lead your service and defend the nation in seamless union with officers of all services. In so doing, you willingly take your place in an ancient and honorable calling, obligated equally to those who have gone before you, those you walk among, and those who will follow.

"There is no greater demonstration of the trust of the Republic than in its expression and bestowal of an officer's commission."[1] This trust involves the majesty of the nation's authority in matters involving the lives and deaths of its citizens. That this particular trust most often is first directed on men and women of no particular experience in life, leadership, or war, elevates the act to a supreme occasion of faith as well. Accepting an officer's commission in the armed forces is a weighty matter, carrying a corresponding burden of practical and moral responsibility. The officer must live up to this responsibility each day he or she serves.

In 1950, the Office of the Secretary of Defense published a small handbook with a dark blue cover titled simply, *The Armed Forces Officer.*[2] Journalist-historian Brigadier General (Army Reserve) S. L. A. Marshall was the author. According to an introduction written by Marshall for a later edition, the Secretary of Defense, General George C. Marshall, "inspired the undertaking due to his personal conviction that American military officers, of whatever service, should share common ground ethically and morally."[3] Defining that common ground, then, became Brigadier General Marshall's goal.

The 1950 edition of *The Armed Forces Officer* is considered something of a classic by many and still deserves close reading. For many years it was presented to new officers on their commissioning. Brigadier General Marshall revised the book several times, through 1975.[4] Following S. L. A. Marshall's death in 1979, Brian P. McMahon, Sr. and John Causten Currey drafted a 1988 edition with advice from an advisory board of retired flag officers.[5] The world has changed dramatically since 1988, politically, technologically, and, therefore, militarily. It is time for another edition of this classic work.

In fall 2002, at a conference on character development and education organized by the U.S. Naval Academy's Center for the Study of Professional Military Ethics and sponsored by Senator and Mrs. John McCain, one line of discussion addressed the possibility of initiating an effort uniting all the service academies to define what it means to be a commissioned officer in the twenty-first century. Within days, the Army Forces Command Commander, General Larry Ellis, suggested to the Commandant of Cadets at West Point that it was time for the Military Academy to take a hand in revising Marshall's old book, which, said Ellis, he still kept on his desk and referred to frequently. With that coincidence of events, the effort to write a new edition of *The Armed Forces Officer* was taken in hand. Three academy superintendents agreed to a joint effort and the Joint Staff J7 agreed to provide sponsorship for what was intended to be a true joint service venture. The Marine Corps University and Coast Guard Academy subsequently came aboard.

This book is written while our nation is at war. It is composed with the belief that the obligations of officership in the armed forces remain timeless and that nothing seen in the war on terrorism, or the campaigns in Afghanistan and Iraq, have indicated otherwise. Indeed, the highly publicized instances of soldier misconduct, such as the disgraceful incidents of prisoner abuse at Abu Ghraib prison and elsewhere, have tended to underscore the importance of active, competent and highly moral-ethical commissioned leadership, precisely by its absence.

The decision was made early in the drafting process to write a new book for the new century while retaining the original title and motivation. The intent is to draft a handbook aimed at new officers and those who aspire to become officers. There is an added ambition that the volume will be sufficiently useful so that it will be retained throughout a career and, like Marshall's original, referred to periodically by senior officers who want to seek renewed inspiration or professional centering. It is the authors' purpose to write the book in the spirit of George C. Marshall's goal: to define the common ethical core of all officers while acknowledging that the military services retain cultural differences that are not only useful to their separate functions but necessary to their common success. Like the nation, the American military forces gain strength from their diversity. *E pluribus unum,*

"From Many, One," could be the motto of the Department of Defense as well as the United States.

All armed forces officers begin their careers taking a common oath and receiving from their constitutional commander in chief a common commission. This oath and the commission, which constitute an individual moral commitment and common executive instruction, are the basis of the common ethic of commissioned leadership that binds the American military into the most effective and loyal fighting force in service to a democracy anywhere. Together they provide the common ethical grounding in which George C. Marshall believed. According to the Air Force Academy Superintendent, service as an officer is a privilege—"a privilege, founded on integrity, that brings with it great responsibility."[6]

An oath is a moral undertaking, "a pledge to perform an act faithfully and truthfully."[7] It commits the oath-taker to do certain things: to tell the truth in criminal trials and to provide disciplined service in the case of military enlistment. According to Admiral Arleigh Burke:

> When an officer swears to "support and defend the Constitution of the United States against all enemies, foreign and domestic"—he [or she] is assuming the most formidable obligation he [or she] will ever encounter in his life. Thousands upon thousands of men and women have died to preserve for him the opportunity to take such an oath. What he [or she] is actually doing is pledging his [or her] means, his [or her] talent, his [or her] very life to his country.[8]

The officer's oath has its origin in the constitutional requirement that "all executive and judicial officers both of the United States and of the several States, shall be bound by oath or affirmation, to support this Constitution...."[9] The current form of the oath dates from the end of the period of Reconstruction (May 1884) when former Confederate officials were readmitted to federal service.[10] All commissioned officers of all military services subscribe to the same oath of office as do other government officials (the president excepted)[11] in a form prescribed under Title 5 of the U.S. Code. Tendered a commission, they swear:

> that I will support and defend the Constitution of the United States against all enemies, foreign and domestic; that I will bear true faith and allegiance to the same; that I take this obligation freely, without any mental reservation or purpose of evasion; and that I will well and faithfully discharge the duties of the office on which I am about to enter. So help me God.

The oath is simple and deliberately unconditional. It is to the Constitution, the legal compact that created our current system of government, designating the president as commander in chief of the Army and Navy[12] (and by extension Air Force, Marine Corps and Coast Guard), while reserving to the Congress the power (and initiative) to raise and support Armies, to provide and maintain a Navy and to make rules for the government of the land and naval forces.[13] Notably, the Constitution explicitly took for granted the existence of state militias that might be called into federal service and thus fall under federal authority. Militias were established, governed, trained, and equipped by the several states. The oath thus acknowledges that the Constitution divides authority over military forces between the federal government and the states, and among the legislative, executive, and judicial branches of the federal government. It requires that individual loyalty focus on the governing compact and thus the rule of law, not on any person or office.

The new officer swears, then, "to well and faithfully discharge the duties of his or her office." To well and faithfully discharge depends not simply on complying with the technical and legal requirements of the office, but also on being consistent with the nation's ideals, fundamental notions of respect for human dignity that are laid down in the Declaration of Independence, the Constitution, and other historic national documents. Officers' understanding of their obligations must extend beyond the letter of the law to the spirit that inspires it.

Having sworn allegiance and loyalty to the Constitution, and good and faithful service, the officer receives a commission from the president of the United States. In contrast to the oath, which has changed several times, the form of the commission is largely unchanged since the Revolutionary War.[14]

The commission defines the station of the officer.

To all who shall see these presents greeting: Know ye that, reposing special trust and confidence in the patriotism, valor, fidelity and abilities of____ _____, I do appoint him a _____(rank)_____ in the (United States Army/Navy/Marine Corps/Air Force/Coast Guard) to rank as such from the __ day of__. This officer will therefore carefully and diligently discharge the duties of the office to which appointed by doing and performing all manner of things thereunto belonging. And I do strictly charge and require those officers and other personnel of lesser rank to render such obedience as is due an officer of this grade and position. And this officer is to observe and follow such orders and directions, from time to time, as may be given by the President of the United States of America, or other superior officers acting in accordance with the laws of the United States of America. This commission is to continue in force during the pleasure of the President of the United States of America under the provisions of those public laws relating to officers of the Armed Forces of the United States of America and the component thereof in which this appointment is made.

The commission is both a letter of instruction and a grant of authority from the president, as commander in chief, to every officer. Officers are commissioned in their individual service, but each commission is otherwise the same. The commission begins by declaring that the officer possesses the special trust and confidence of the president in the appointee's patriotism, valor, fidelity, and abilities—his or her love of country, moral and physical courage under threat, faithfulness in thought and action, and professional competence.

Where the oath of office requires the officer to swear that he or she will well and faithfully discharge the duties of the office, the commission commands the new officer "to carefully and diligently discharge the duties of the office to which appointed. ..." The president charges subordinates to obey the orders of the officer, and the officer to comply with the instructions and directives of the president and superior officers, notably limiting this responsibility to those officials "acting in accordance with the laws of the United States of America." Even presidential orders, then, are no defense for American officers acting outside the law. Finally, the commission makes it clear that the officer, like all officials of the executive branch of government, serves at the pleasure of the president.

Everything in this book about the nature of the officer can be said to derive from the oath of office, the commission, the military provisions of the Constitution, its enabling legislation, and the inherent nature of the military calling.

Chapter 1 reminds us that American armed forces officers are citizen-soldiers, recounting sublime moments of self-sacrifice for the nation, which mark what journalist William Pfaff referred to as "the honorable absurdity of the soldier's role ... an undertaking to offer one's life, and to assume the right to take the lives of others."[15] Chapter 2 describes the profession of arms and the central role the warrior-leader will continue to play even as the practical nature of warfare undergoes rapid change. The warrior ethos remains at the center of a twenty-first century officer's calling. Chapter 3 is a consideration of a key contextual factor of an officer's service that all American officers are expected to perform as leader-members of honored professions, their individual services, and, as joint service officers, as members of smoothly functioning, integrated, multiservice teams.

Chapter 4 addresses the requirement, central to the oath of every Soldier, Sailor, Airman, Coast Guardsman, or Marine, to defend the Constitution, and the role of every armed forces officer to be a servant of the nation. Chapter 5 examines the moral requirement that every officer be a leader of character and display a nobility of life and action to live up to the nation's expectations and make the officer an inspirational leader for others to follow. Chapter 6 discusses leadership for new officers. Chapter 7, "Responsibility, Accountability, and Discipline," addresses that which most distinguishes commissioned officers from other categories of military leader—what S. L. A. Marshall referred to as their exceptional and unremitting responsibility.[16] Chapter 8, "Service Identity and Joint Warfighting," seeks to establish a balance between the twin goods of the unique service cultures and the imperative for all services to come together as one cohesive, unified force on the battlefield. Finally, Chapter 9 summarizes what it means to be a member in an ancient and honorable calling, the commissioned leadership of the profession of arms, in the twenty-first century.

There are several appendices. These contain the nation's founding documents; the sections of Title 10, U.S. Code that establish the several services; a compendium of service values; The Code of Conduct; and a discussion of those things new officers should be aware of titled, "Keeping Your House in Order."[17] The first chapter of S. L. A. Marshall's first edition is included as the final appendix. Marshall's language is a bit dated, but the chapter retains its original ability to inspire officers of all generations alike. The final element is a list, compiled by the authors of this book, of recommended books that might provide the foundations of an armed forces officer's professional library.

Officers and civilian faculty members from each of the service academies drafted this book.[18] In the spirit of *E pluribus unum*, only modest efforts have been made to smooth the individual voices and styles. We adopt the current convention of capitalizing the titles of members of the armed forces: Soldier, Sailor, Marine, Airman, and Coast Guardsman. Where we have not, as in the first chapter, the word "Soldier" is taken to comprehend members of all services. Our use of quotations is based on the value and authority of the argument put forward. For purposes of inclusion, we have introduced into some the feminine pronouns in brackets, excepting only those, as in the reverse of the title page, where it would have done excessive violence to the text. Both men and women serve as equals in the armed forces today. Both pay the inevitable costs of war in risk of life and limb. We believe our text should reflect an equivalent equality of respect.

1. Colonel John R. Allen, USMC, Commandant of Midshipmen, USNA, "Commander's Intent," 19 December 2002.

2. U.S. Department of Defense, *The Armed Forces Officer* (Washington, DC: Government Printing Office, 1950). The identity of the author was not given in the original edition.

3. U.S. Department of Defense, *The Armed Forces Officer* (Washington, DC: Armed Forces Information Service, 1975), ii. S. L. A. Marshall contributed a signed Introduction to the 1975 edition explaining how he happened to write the book.

4. The 1950 edition was reprinted in 1956 as Department of the Army Pamphlet 660-2. It was revised in 1960 as DOD Pam 1-20/DA Pam 600-2/NAVPERS 15923A/ AFP 190-1-12/NAVMC 2563 and again in 1975 as DOD GEN-36/ DA Pam 600-2/NAVEDTRA 46905/AFP 190-13/NAVMC-2563 (Rev 75).

5. Available from the Secretary of the Army's Public Affairs Office at: http://www.usapa.army.mil/pdffiles/p600_2.pdf, on-line, Internet, 18 May 2004.

6. Lieutenant General John W. Rosa, Superintendent, U.S. Air Force Academy, preface to U.S. Air Force Academy, Officer Development System, January 2004, 1.

7. Lieutenant Colonel Thomas Reese, "An Officer's Oath," *Military Law Review*, 25 (1 July 1964): 3.

8. Admiral Arleigh Burke, USN (Ret.), quoted in ibid., 39.

9. Article VI. The officer's oath is found in Government Organization and Employees (Title V) U.S. Code, Section 3331.

10. To be precise, the current form was adopted in 1862 in response to the loss of a large number of army officers to the Confederacy. The oath was streamlined to its current form in 1884. Reese, "An Officer's Oath," 9-10. See also, Edward M. Coffman, "The Army Officer and the Constitution," *Parameters* 17, no. 3 (September 1987): 2-12. Another account of the history of the officer's oath is Lieutenant Colonel Kenneth Keskel, USAF, "The Oath of Office: A Historical Guide to Moral Leadership," *Air & Space Power Journal* 16, no. 4 (Winter 2002), on-line, Internet, 18 May 2004, available from http://www.airpower.maxwell.af.mil/airchronicles/apj/apj02/win02/ keskel.html.

11. The president's Oath alone is given in the Constitution, Article II, Section 1. The president swears to "preserve, protect and defend the Constitution."

12. Article II, Section 2.

13. Article I, Section 8.

14. See the form used in the Revolutionary War in the George Washington Papers at the Library of Congress, 1741-1799, Series 4, General Correspondence, 1677-1799, Continental Congress, 1777, Printed Commission Form, Image 676 of 1269, on-line, Internet, 18 May 2004, available from http://memory.loc.gov/cgi-bin/query/P?mgw: 11:./temp/~ammem_pZij. One major change, of course, is the presence of the president as commander in chief under the constitutional system. During the Revolution, Congress granted commissions.

15. William Pfaff, "The Honorable Absurdity of the Soldier's Role," *The International Herald Tribune Online* (March 25, 2003), on-line, Internet, 25 March 2003, available from http://www.iht.com/ihtsearch.php?id=90840&owner=(IHT)&date=200303261 63223.

16. *The Armed Forces Officer* (1950), 2.

17. S. L. A. Marshall always included such a chapter in his versions of the book.

18. A list of the authors and their organizational affiliations while they worked on it is included at the end of this book.

CHAPTER 1

THE CITIZEN-SOLDIER—AN AMERICAN TRADITION OF MILITARY SERVICE

From the birth of democracy in ancient Greece, the idea of the citizen-soldier has been the single most important factor to shape the Western way of war. In a democracy, combatants bear arms as equals, fighting to defend their ideals and way of life. They are citizens with a stake in the society they have vowed to defend. They do not fight as mercenaries, nor are they guided by coercion or allegiance to the whims of a dictatorial leader. Rather, their motivation stems from a selfless commitment to an idea that far exceeds the interests of any individual member of the society.[1] For the armed forces officer of the United States, this ethos began with the militiamen who defended their homes, secured the frontier, and won a war of independence against the most formidable military power of that era. The American military tradition has since been governed by a strict adherence to the primacy of civilian control and, within that framework, has continued to champion the role of the citizen-soldier as the defender of the nation's ideals.

In Congress, 4 July 1776, the founders of our nation outlined what they described as "self-evident" truths—universal principles concerning the proper relationship between citizens and government. Human rights, quantified as "life, liberty, and the pursuit of happiness," were their foremost concern, and government's primary purpose was to defend those rights for all citizens. This definition of government radically transformed the role of the military in society. As the Declaration of Independence insisted, kings could no longer regard their armies as "independent of" or "superior to" civilian interests. From now on, rulers and military officers themselves would be subject to the will of the people. The priority of human rights, endowed by the Creator, would serve as the new focal point of allegiance for all citizens, whether civilian or military. From the outset, the American vision required military officers to serve first and foremost as citizens of the nation, embodying the very ideals they swore to defend.

The American Civil War tested the resolve of the American citizen-soldier like no other crisis in our nation's history. Christmas 1860 revealed an increasingly difficult period for the Corps of Cadets at West Point. Divided over the looming national crisis, most Southern cadets had already submitted their resignations, and more were sure to follow. With the Christmas season in view, the cadets of West Point gathered in the chapel and sang a hymn usually reserved for the last chapel service before graduation, "When Shall We Meet Again." In December 1860, the words of the hymn suddenly alerted the cadets to what serving the nation might truly entail.

> When shall we meet again?
> Meet ne'er to sever?
> When will Peace wreath her chain
> Round us forever?
> Our hearts will ne'er repose
> Safe from each blast that blows
> In this dark vale of woes, —
> Never—no, never.[2]

Over the next four years, former cadet roommates, now serving as commissioned officers in blue and gray, would face the impossible challenge of fighting one another on opposing sides to determine the destiny of the United States of America. The aftermath would reaffirm the resolve of federal principles established in the Constitution of 1789 and redefine the very oath of the armed forces officer. No longer pledging to bear allegiance only to the United States, officers after 1862 would take an oath to support and defend the Constitution.[3] In this fashion, the oath unmistakably underscored "We the People" as the highest authority in the military chain of command.

As soldier and citizen, today's armed forces officer is a champion of both the nation's defense and the principles upon which the nation was founded. Taking an oath to support and defend the Constitution means swearing to uphold the core values that define the essence of American citizenship; the armed forces officer is first and foremost a citizen who has embraced the ideals of the nation—only then can he or she defend those principles with true conviction.

It was an unswerving sense of civic responsibility that ultimately led Joshua Lawrence Chamberlain to Gettysburg in 1863. During that battle, Chamberlain, a professor of modern languages from Bowdoin College, led his 20th Maine Volunteers in a courageous stand against Confederate assault and secured the southern end of the Union line at Little Round Top.[4] Colonel Chamberlain epitomized the ideal of the citizen-soldier, not only for his decisive leadership in battle, but for his commitment to the principles for which he felt called to join the defense of the Union. In his view, right action left the North no other option than to preserve the Union. As a professor watching the young men from his classes enlist in the army, Chamberlain was burdened with a sense of duty and responsibility yet unfulfilled. Despite opposition from his wife and colleagues, the 33-year-old professor made the decision that would redefine his life's mission. In response to the personal request of the governor of Maine to accept the leadership of a new regiment, Chamberlain wrote, "I feel it to be my duty to serve my Country. Your call to a post of honorable service finds me as a good citizen to come forward without delay & without excuse… I can make no other decision."[5]

For the armed forces officer, it is not enough to be willing to support the ideas of the Constitution or even be willing to give one's life in their defense. As the nation's trusted professionals trained in the art and application of war, we are held to a higher standard—we are required to embody the values we have taken an oath to defend. At the end of the Civil War, Joshua Chamberlain, having been promoted to brigadier general, demonstrated that commitment during the surrender of Robert E. Lee's forces at Appomattox Court House. Having given much thought to how he should lead his men to respond to the weary ranks of Confederate Soldiers, Chamberlain resolved to show respect to the defeated enemy by having his men present a salute of arms. Although he anticipated harsh criticism from his superiors for this gesture of respect, Chamberlain stated that "nothing of that kind could move me in the least. … Before us in proud humiliation stood the embodiment of manhood … thin, worn, and famished, but erect, and with eyes looking level into ours, waking memories that bound us together as no other bond—was not such manhood to be welcomed back into a Union so tested and assured?"[6] Sixty years later, a Virginian who had been among the Confederates that day asserted that the healing of the nation "began with that order to present arms."[7] Given the choice between exacting revenge and upholding justice, Chamberlain followed a path guided by principle, even when bitterness and war-weariness urged otherwise. In so doing, he paid tribute to the more than 600,000 that made the ultimate sacrifice during the war, but more importantly, Chamberlain reflected the very ideals for which those thousands had shed their blood.

As military officers, we have taken an oath of service above and beyond the ordinary parameters of noble citizenship. Our role in "promoting the general welfare" ultimately requires an unflinching commitment to service before self. In some cases, we may be required to sacrifice our very lives. Countless numbers of American citizen-soldiers have had to make this choice, and as the next generation of armed forces officers, we have volunteered to inherit that legacy and selflessly perform our service to the nation. In this light, courage is not a matter of heroism or extraordinary strength, but of inner conviction and faith—the decision to do the right thing for the right reason, no matter the cost.

During the opening stages of the Battle of Midway, 4 June 1942, Lieutenant Commander John Waldron and his squadron of 15 TBD-1 Devastators had just taken off from the aircraft carrier USS *Hornet* at 0806.[8] They were headed southeast over the Pacific in search of the Japanese fleet. Originally from Pierre, South Dakota, Lieutenant Commander Waldron, "the Skipper," was described by his fellow naval officers as "a regular guy" who was "loyal and thoughtful, and tough."[9] The night before, Waldron had written a letter to his wife that stated, "I believe that we will be in battle very soon. I wish we were there today. But, as we are up to the very eve of serious business, I wish to record to you that I am feeling fine … my place is here with the fight. I could not be happy otherwise … if I do not come back, well, you and the little girls can know that this squadron struck for the highest objective in Naval warfare—to sink the enemy."[10]

As a commander, Waldron's character, sense of urgency, and concern for his men inspired the 15 junior pilots and 15 radio-gunners of Torpedo Squadron Eight to prepare for battle with courage and conviction. Most of the Airmen were green, and all except Waldron were novices when it came to the mission—even up until the Midway battle, none of the pilots had the chance to practice taking off with a torpedo, let alone dropping one in the water.[11] Handling aircraft, machine guns, and radios as proficiently as he did his acclaimed six-shooter, Waldron did his best to train Torpedo Eight in every facet of the mission: "Someday, you'll be out there in the Pacific, and you'll be all alone, and there won't be any gals to cheer you on … your nerve won't pull you out then. By golly, you are going to know what to do. … I've been in that sort of jam and it's that sort of sixth sense that saved my life."[12] Waldron's definition of heroism hinged on the principle that ordinary men could prepare to meet the enemy in extraordinary fashion. His pilots knew him first and foremost as a patriot who loved his country—courage and sacrifice were, in his view, the highest expressions of citizenship.

With an uncanny intuition for the enemy's next move, Waldron led his torpedomen straight to the pride of Admiral Nagumo's carrier task force—*Akagi*, *Kaga*, *Hiryu*, and *Soryu*. At 0918, the carriers had just finished landing airplanes returning from their initial strikes on Midway Island.[13] Waldron gave the signal for the torpedo bombers to line up for an attack on the largest carrier. However, the Japanese had already been alerted to the presence of the U.S. carriers, and the Zeros were airborne, ready to head off Waldron's Devastators. With no fighter support to divert the Zeros, the torpedo bombers were flying into a trap, alone and vastly outnumbered. There was nowhere to run.[14] Recognizing the opportunity to disrupt the landing and regeneration of further Japanese aircraft, Waldron broke radio silence and stated firmly, "WE WILL GO IN. WE WON'T TURN BACK. FORMER STRATEGY CANNOT BE USED. WE WILL ATTACK. GOOD LUCK!"[15] As machine-gun bullets began to rip into the formation, the torpedo bombers held their descent and lined up on their targets to get their "fish" in the water. After a few of the torpedo bombers had been hit, Waldron's plane burst into flames. In an effort to escape the blazing heat, his wingman saw Waldron place his right leg outside the cockpit just before his aircraft plunged into the water and disappeared.[16]

At the end of the hour, every plane from Torpedo Squadron Eight had been lost, and only one of 30 valiant crewmembers lived to tell the story. Not a single torpedo that splashed into the water ever hit a target, but Waldron's squadron did manage to disrupt Japanese preparations long enough to give follow-on aircraft from *Yorktown* and *Enterprise* opportunity to destroy *Akagi*, *Kaga*, and *Soryu* within the next few hours.[17]

According to pilot George Gay, the sole survivor of Torpedo Eight, the key to understanding John Waldron "is not what happened, but why he did what he did that day." Before departing *Hornet*, Waldron had told his crews he expected the Battle of Midway would be the "biggest of the war, and may well be the turning point." In the ready room, Waldron carefully prepared a mimeographed statement which he had each of his men read silently: "MY GREATEST HOPE IS THAT WE ENCOUNTER A FAVORABLE TACTICAL SITUATION, BUT IF WE DON'T AND WORST COMES TO WORST, I WANT EACH OF US TO DO HIS UTMOST TO DESTROY OUR ENEMIES. IF THERE IS ONLY ONE PLANE LEFT TO MAKE FINAL RUN-IN, I WANT THAT MAN TO GO IN AND GET A HIT."[18] Waldron's focus was more than mission execution. Armed with an uncommon sense of conviction and patriotic zeal, he was committed to the principle of doing the right thing for the right reason. He embodied the Constitutional ideal of self-sacrifice, finding the resolve to lay his life on the line to promote the welfare of the nation. Waldron demonstrated that for citizen-soldiers, heroism is a function of our faith and conviction to give all we have for something we believe in.

An officer is granted an enormous responsibility to make decisions and lead others into combat. The values we have sworn to protect and defend represent a distinct perspective, faith, and conviction that require commitment beyond mere mental assent. Service to the nation requires us to embody self-sacrifice in every facet of our character and conduct, and it provides the essential reference point for how we execute our mission. As citizen-soldiers, we have not only committed ourselves to safeguard a set of ideals, we have accepted the higher responsibility of serving as their chief promoters, both at home and abroad. If necessary, we are willing to lay down our lives in their defense.

In the 1950s, like many boys from small Midwestern towns, Lance Peter Sijan was a Boy Scout who sang in the church choir, earned his own spending money, and used his model airplanes to dream of future adventures in the sky. In his Milwaukee high school, he excelled in academics, lettered in football, and carried a reputation for honesty and genuine commitment to others that followed him through his officer training at the Air Force Academy where he graduated as a second lieutenant in 1965.

On the evening of 9 November 1967, 25-year-old Lieutenant Sijan was on his 53rd combat mission in Vietnam. He was the back-seater in an F-4 scheduled for another bomb run on the Ho Chi Minh Trail in Laos. Not unlike other pilots flying out of South Vietnam, Lance wrestled with the frustration of targeting the same ambiguous patch of jungle, using the same call sign and time-on-target as in previous night missions. These flights seemingly exposed aircrews to an inordinate level of risk for little gain. One of his F-4 pilot roommates recalled that "Lance had discussed these tactical shortcomings, necessitated by the wider policy considerations of limited war. But he still wore his uniform with pride every day, and refused to denigrate the national policy."[19]

As orange tracer fire ruptured the night sky, Sijan pressed the button to jettison his bomb load. An electronic malfunction detonated the bombs upon release, suddenly engulfing his Phantom in flames. Sijan ejected and drifted into the densely forested jungle below. His was the only chute known to emerge from the fireball.[20]

Sijan regained consciousness the next day, suffering from acute lacerations, a crushed right hand, a compound fracture in his left leg, and head injuries. A flight of F-4s intercepted Sijan's beeper and a search and rescue effort commenced. However, just as the Jolly Green chopper arrived at the pickup point, North Vietnamese Army (NVA) gunners entered the area. Sijan's voice came over the radio, "The enemy is too close... stay where you are—I'll crawl to the penetrator."[21] Unable to move his injured body fast enough through the jungle foliage, darkness and weakened radio batteries prevented further rescue coordination. Able only to inch himself along the ground on his back, Sijan evaded capture for 45 days. His strength severely depleted, he managed to move some three miles from his starting position before the North Vietnamese discovered his unconscious, skeletal form in the middle of the Ho Chi Minh Trail.[22] After awakening in an NVA road camp, Sijan mustered enough strength to overpower one of his guards and crawl into the jungle. However, he was recaptured after several hours, beaten severely, and taken along with two other U.S. pilots to the Hoa Lo Prison in Hanoi.

Lance Sijan would never have considered himself to be a hero. However, his commitment as a citizen-soldier to the Constitutional principles he vowed to defend led him to conduct himself in an extraordinarily heroic manner. "He was dedicated to being a good pilot, a true professional, he had the self-discipline to recognize the hard duty he had as a downed pilot ... to escape and evade."[23] For Sijan, freedom was more than the anticipated hope of returning home—it was an idea that Sijan had sworn as an officer to fight for, even to lay his life down for. "He knew exactly what he was doing and why."[24]

Throughout his captivity, Sijan continuously resisted torture and refused to provide any military information to his captors. While enduring the chill of his damp prison cell, Sijan contracted pneumonia. With an iron will that refused to accept defeat, he instructed his cellmates to prop him up such that he might exercise his arms to condition himself for an escape attempt. A fighter until the end, Sijan died in prison on 22 January 1968.

Ultimately, Lance Sijan was a champion of the nation's ideals, not because he took an oath to defend them, but because he believed in them. They were at the core of his very being. In his drive to evade capture and resist the enemy, Sijan demonstrated his unwavering commitment to the principle of freedom. He never anticipated on that fateful evening of November 1967 that his crippled F-4 would suddenly place him in the direst of survival situations. But Lance acted with honor because his convictions made it impossible for him to do otherwise. Glenn Nordin was the Jolly Green chopper pilot who heard Sijan's last transmission during the failed rescue attempt. According to Nordin, "Sijan was in control of himself under the worst possible conditions. He had not only been courageous during his long struggle, he had been imaginative, cunning. ... The ability to make hard but necessary decisions under difficult conditions, then to show the strength of character to implement those decisions, despite hardship, despite resistance, both in combat and times of peace."[25]

The pride of our nation's armed services stands on the shoulders of countless young men and women from all walks of life who have sworn to support and defend the ideals that define the essence of our American citizenship. In the same way Japanese aircraft over Pearl Harbor in 1941 galvanized the resolve of a nation, the September 11th terrorist attacks on the World Trade Center and Pentagon in 2001 reminded us of the difficult sacrifices required to sustain our Constitutional freedoms. The global war on terrorism ushered the U. S. military into groundbreaking expeditionary efforts and prolonged stability operations designed to replace rogue regimes with representative governments while winning the hearts and minds of civilian populations harassed by insurgents. In this arena, armed forces officers stood on the front lines of both a military and an ideological battlefield, serving as ambassadors of democracy and the Constitutional principles embodied in their service as citizen-soldiers. Global commitments especially underscored the extent to which Reserve Components, serving alongside their active duty counterparts, were essential in sustaining our military capabilities. Extended tours and subsequent rotations into and out of the combat zones called for uncommon courage and perseverance in the face of asymmetric warfare in urban environments and prolonged separations from families back home. In the twenty-first century, more than ever, the ideal of the citizen-soldier remains at the core of the American military service tradition.

Unlike those who made the ultimate sacrifice in a singular act of military heroism, Captain Bill Jacobsen was killed when a suicide bomber entered his mess tent in Mosul on 21 December 2004. He was 31 years old, and the fateful attack occurred on his ninth wedding anniversary, taking his life along with five of the light-armored Stryker Brigade troops he commanded in Iraq.

From his youth, Jacobsen had always planned to serve in the Army; he was an Army brat who became an Eagle Scout and graduated from Brigham Young

University with an ROTC commission in 1998. He was a marathon runner who also enjoyed scuba diving and mountain biking. The devoted father of four decorated the tiny space he called home in Iraq with pictures of his wife and children. Deployed less than three months in Mosul, the 184 men he commanded trusted his leadership in urban warfare, witnessed his diplomatic skill in working with the local population, and observed how he prayed before each meal in the mess tent. He built a strong rapport with his troops and instilled a sense of confidence through his conviction in the democratic ideals he believed would prevail against even the most bitter Sunni neighborhoods; "It was the small details—the signs of respect, the signals that soldiers view fighting as a last option—that would help make the difference."[26]

Jacobsen's father, a retired lieutenant colonel and Vietnam veteran, described his son as an officer who fully embraced the mission in Iraq; "He felt we are blessed in this country with the freedoms that we have ... this was something he believed in. ... He felt like he had a responsibility to help people gain freedom and democracy."[27] Like many countless citizen-soldiers before him, Captain Jacobsen served because he knew freedom never comes without a price. His seemingly random death at the hand of a suicide bomber reminds us that heroism is not defined so much by the capacity in which someone serves, but by the convictions that compel someone to place themselves in harm's way. Captain Jacobsen gave his life not only for his country, but for the principles he had embraced and deemed worthy of the ultimate sacrifice.[28]

The United States Constitution calls on all citizens to "establish Justice, insure domestic Tranquility, provide for the common defense, promote the general Welfare, and secure the Blessings of Liberty to ourselves and our Posterity." As citizen-soldiers, the armed forces of the United States have the privilege of defending those ideals against enemies foreign and domestic—in the process, we are the standard bearers for those very principles. As exemplified by Joshua Chamberlain, John Waldron, Lance Sijan, and Bill Jacobsen, officers are advocates of justice, self-sacrifice, and freedom. Proudly, we represent a cross-section of American society from all walks of life. We achieve promotions and leadership positions based on merit and proven ability to lead. Our strength is our common commitment to a democratic ideal that requires us to view one another as equals. When we serve together in combat, this democratic faith enables us to depend on each other for our very lives, and even more importantly, for the defense of our nation and the principles it represents.

1. Victor Davis Hanson, *Courage and Culture: Landmark Battles in the Rise of Western Power* (New York: Doubleday, 2001), 3-8.
2. Ibid.
3. Lieutenant Colonel Kenneth Keskel, "The Oath of Office: A Historical Guide to Moral Leadership," *Air & Space Power Journal* 16 (Winter 2002): 50.
4. Edward Longarce, *Joshua Chamberlain: The Soldier and the Man* (Conshohocken, PA: Combined Publishers, 1999).
5. Mark Nesbitt, *Through Blood and Fires: Selected Civil War Papers of Major General Joshua Chamberlain* (Mechanicsburg, PA: Stackpole Books, 1996), 14.
6. Longarce, *Joshua Chamberlain*, 246.
7. Ibid., 247.
8. Walter Lord, *Incredible Victory* (New York: Harper and Row, 1967), 140-141.
9. George Gay, *Sole Survivor: The Battle of Midway and its Effects on his Life* (Naples, FL: Midway Publishers, 1980), 305, 308.
10. Ibid., 109.
11. Ibid., 117.
12. Ibid., 95-96.
13. Gordon W. Prange, *Miracle at Midway* (New York: McGraw Hill, 1982), 232-246.
14. Gay, *Sole Survivor*, 119.
15. Ibid., 119.
16. Ibid., 121.
17. Edward Jablonski, *Airwar: An Illustrated History of Air Power in the Second World War* (New York: Doubleday, 1979), 92-95.
18. Ibid., 108.
19. Malcolm McConnell, *Into the Mouth of the Cat: The Story of Lance Sijan, Hero of Vietnam* (New York: W.W. Norton, 1985), 228.
20. John L. Frisbee, "Lance Sihan's Incredible Journey," *Air Force Magazine*, December 1986, 116.
21. McConnell, 234.
22. Frisbee, "Sijan's Incredible Journey," 116.
23. Ibid.
24. McConnell, 231.
25. Ibid., 234.
26. Richard A. Oppel, Jr., "A Faith in Quiet Diplomacy, Giving Respect, to the end," *The New York Times*, 2 January 2005.
27. Sam Skolnik, "Capt William W, Jacobsen Jr.: Captain has a strong belief in democracy," *Seattle Post Intelligencer*, 25 December 2004.
28. Lauren Graf et al., "At Least 6 Fort Lewis soldiers are among Mosul dead," *The Seattle Times*, 24 December 2004.

CHAPTER 2

THE PROFESSION OF ARMS

Humans fight as individuals and as groups. Some fight primarily for money, some for love of fighting, and some for lack of alternative opportunities. "From the beginning of ... recorded history physical force, or the threat of it, has always been freely applied to the resolution of social problems."[1] Human societies— from tribes and city-states to empires, organized religions, and nation-states— have regularly established and relied on groups of specialists who, willingly or unwillingly, assumed the burden of fighting, killing, and dying for the larger group. Whatever their formal name or title, theirs is the profession of arms.

It is a basic premise of civilized societies, especially democratic ones, that the military serves the state (and by extension, the people), not the other way around. The profession of arms exists to serve the larger community, to help accomplish its purposes and objectives, and to protect its way of life. "The justification for the maintenance and employment of military force [or military forces, for that matter] is the political ends of the state."[2] In wartime or in peacetime, at home or abroad, the armed forces serve the larger society and perform the tasks their government assigns them. "The function of the profession of arms is the ordered application of force in the resolution of a social or political problem."[3] The essential task of its members is to fight, individually and collectively; of its officers, to direct and lead those who apply the instruments of destruction to achieve assigned ends. With rare exceptions, a society's government identifies the problems to be resolved with force, and it then turns to and relies on the professionals to handle the always difficult, usually dangerous, often bloody details in a manner acceptable to the citizens and supportive of their goals.

The most basic task of the profession of arms is the armed defense of the society, its territory, population, and vital interests. In its most elemental sense, the profession of arms is all about fighting and all about war. As the nineteenth-century Prussian strategist and student of war Carl von Clausewitz observed, "for as long as they practice this activity, soldiers will think of themselves as members

---

of a kind of guild, in whose regulations, laws, and customs the spirit of war is given pride of place."[4] The defining mission of the armed forces is the preparation for and the conduct of war, which includes securing the military victory until peace is restored politically. It is the warfighting mission that determines how they are organized, equipped, and trained.

However, defense of self and of others does not exhaust the tasks societies give their organized warriors. Because they are disciplined and armed organizations with a wide range of skills and capabilities, military forces are called upon frequently to perform other important missions in service to the state, such as maintaining civil order at home and abroad and providing disparate forms of civil relief in times of crisis. In the United States, the Army, in particular, has been used at various times for internal development, as well as to promote exploration, to maintain order, to enforce federal law, and even to run Civilian Conservation Corps camps during the Great Depression of the 1930s. The U.S. Coast Guard's principal roles involve maintaining the security and safety of the nation's ports and waterways and enforcing federal laws and treaties on the high seas. It is important not to confuse the primary mission for which armed forces are created, trained, and equipped, with a limitation on the range of missions society may give them. They are expected to bring great skill and enthusiasm to all assignments.

Whatever its particular forms, the unique and specialized service to the nation gives the military profession its own nature and distinctive status, as well as privileges and responsibilities denied or spared the rest of the society. Because those responsibilities include the potential wholesale taking and losing of life, the military profession stands alone, in its own eyes and in the eyes of those it serves. Its members must always be conscious of their commitment: to be prepared to give, in Lincoln's words, "the last full measure of devotion."[5] They serve at frequent cost to their convenience, their comfort, the stability of their families, and often their limbs and lives. It is ultimately because of their willingness to endure hardship, and risk life and limb on behalf of the nation, not the willingness to kill and destroy in the nation's name, that members of all armed forces enjoy the respect and gratitude of the people they serve. Theirs is a higher loyalty and purpose, or rather a hierarchy of loyalties, which puts nation above service, service above their comrades in arms, and comrades above self. Soldiers serve the nation; they fight and die for each other.

The commitment to the nation is a two-way street—between the individual military member and the larger society. Society invests much—its safety and security, its hopes and ideals, much of its treasure, and the best of its men and women—in the armed forces. For the member of the profession of arms, fulfilling the society's demands and expectations means investing one's best as a professional and as a person. Sir John Hackett observed, "Service under arms has been seen at times and in some places as a calling resembling that of the priesthood in its dedication."[6] Like the priesthood, the profession of arms is a higher calling, to serve others, to sacrifice self, to be about something larger than one's own ambitions and desires, something grander than one's own contributions and even one's own life. As S. L. A. Marshall wrote, "… service to country is no longer a beautiful abstraction; it is the sternly concrete and unremitting obligation of service to the regiment, the squadron, or the ship's company."[7]

This hierarchy of loyalties has several formulations in the United States Armed Forces. In the Air Force it is "service before self." In the Navy it is "ship-shipmate-self." The Army defines the value of loyalty as a hierarchy of responsibilities to Constitution, service, unit, and other Soldiers.[8] The basic idea is that there is always something larger, more important than the individual. Service in the armed forces is not primarily about self, but rather about others—fellow citizens and fellow military members. "The military ethic is corporative in spirit."[9]

The loyalty to fellow military members has its roots and its rationale in the ultimate activity of the armed forces—combat and war. What Lieutenant General (Ret.) Harold G. Moore and Joseph L. Galloway wrote in the prologue to their memorable book about Vietnam could have been said by warriors of any nation about any war: "We discovered in that depressing, hellish place, where death was our constant companion, that we loved each other. We killed for each other, we died for each other, and we wept for each other."[10] The classic statement of this perennial and honorable theme is in Shakespeare's Henry V:

> We few, we happy few, we band of brothers;
> For he today that sheds his blood with me
> Shall be my brother.

Given the stakes, it is no wonder that the profession of arms invokes and requires, in the words of the U.S. military officer's commission, "special trust and confidence."

The profession of arms has two major components within which almost everything else that is important is subsumed. There is a functional component, what the armed forces do, and there is a moral component, what they owe the nation. The two are intimately joined.

The functional component flows from the missions and tasks that a society assigns its armed forces. All professions require competence and mastery of the technical details and techniques essential to and unique to them. The higher the stakes, the greater are the demands and expectations for competence. In matters of life and death, in medicine and the military, for example, the stakes and the standards are especially high. Every military professional learns quickly how complex and demanding this field of endeavor is, in its technological and its human dimensions. Military affairs are about both things and people. The sheer quantity and sophistication of technical details in most military specialties would leave the average civilian awestruck. Almost nothing about the profession of arms is easy—or forgiving. How well the individual practitioner, especially the officer, masters this panoply of skills can determine who lives and who dies—and it often does.

The functional component has two dimensions—individual and organizational. Not only must the officer hone his or her own skills to the sharpest edge, but officership, especially command, which is officership's most essential function, carries the additional burden of responsibility for the collective skills of the organization—as a unit. "It is worth remembering from the start that military practice is group practice. The military art is deeply concerned with the performance of the human group under stress."[11]

While the technical competencies vary greatly from specialty to specialty, even within a warfare specialty or branch, the requirements of the second component—the moral component—are common across the profession of arms and central to it. Vice Admiral James B. Stockdale, Medal of Honor recipient for his service under the arduous conditions of long incarceration and torture as a prisoner of war, a timeless exemplar of moral military leadership, summed it up well: "Morality lurks in all the shadows surrounding our profession. To not only ignore it but fail to embrace it will ultimately ensure your failure in the … service."[12] Great though the powers of the officer are, especially in command, Stockdale cautioned an audience of future officers, "…even in the most detached duty, we warriors must keep foremost in our minds that there are boundaries to the prerogatives of leadership, moral boundaries."[13] Values limit acceptable actions in peace and war. There are things we do not do.

One way to capture the range of requirements in the moral component is to think about three categories of ethical issues. The first could be called The Individual in the Profession, the second The Profession at Work, and the third The Profession and the Society. The Individual in the Profession consists of those characteristics or virtues required of all military professionals. This is the realm, for example, of Duty, Honor, Country. It is accepted that "[T]he military establishment requires a sense of duty and honor to accomplish its objectives,"[14] and so too do all its members to accomplish theirs. All members of the profession of arms, but most especially officers, must nurture and cultivate this broad set of virtues in order to carry out all their responsibilities successfully and consistently. The profession itself, and the individual service in which one serves, must assume some of the burden of education and support for character formation. At its core, this remains an integral part of the individual's personal obligation and responsibility to well and faithfully execute the duties of the office.

The Profession at Work treats the most important, indeed defining, work of the profession of arms: the conduct of war. The ethics of war are incorporated and embodied in what has been called "The Warrior's Honor."[15]

> While these codes vary from culture to culture, they seem to exist in all cultures, and their common features are among the oldest artifacts of human morality. … As ethical systems, they were primarily concerned with establishing the rules of combat and defining the system of moral etiquette by which warriors judged themselves to be worthy of mutual respect.[16]

The basic notion of the warrior's honor is nearly universal, transcending historical periods and cultures. It serves more than one purpose: distinguishing between those who fight honorably and those who do not, regulating acceptable weapons and practices, defining acceptable treatment of prisoners and the wounded.[17] Men and women who fight under such codes are members of an honorable profession. They are soldiers and warriors, and can proudly call themselves such. But those who fight outside or without such codes are not members of an honorable profession. With no code to bind and inspire them, they are, instead, barbarians or criminals. "For war, unconstrained by honor and high moral principle, is quickly reduced to murder, mayhem, and all the basest tendencies of mankind."[18]

For sons and daughters of the Western heritage, the primary ethical code governing the conduct of war is called the Just War Tradition. This moral tradition has roots in philosophy, theology, law, the practice of statecraft, and military codes such as chivalry. It has two aspects, usually identified by their Latin names: *jus ad bellum*, which informs and guides the decision to go to war, and *jus in bello*, which informs and guides the conduct of war.[19] Members of the armed forces are interested principally in the *jus in bello*, for they are the ones who conduct war.

According to *jus in bello*, for a war to be conducted justly it must meet two basic criteria–discrimination and proportionality. The principle underlying discrimination is noncombatant immunity: noncombatants may never be the object of an intentional direct attack. Noncombatants include not only civilians caught up in the maelstrom of war, but unresisting enemy soldiers who are wounded and out of the fight and those who have surrendered and been taken prisoner. Combatants include not only most military personnel but also civilians actively engaged in the war effort (e.g., delivering ammunition to the front lines or taking up weapons themselves). Proportionality says that the harm done in any military operation should not outweigh the good likely to be accomplished; that is, it must not be disproportionate to the legitimate gains achieved by a military operation.

These principles are so widely accepted that they form the basis of the Law of Armed Conflict. Formalized in international law, ratified in treaties, these principles provide a common ground for distinguishing warriors from barbarians, and honorable soldiers from war criminals. Acts that violate this code offend the human conscience. This notion is deeply embedded in the profession of arms and the American psyche. General of the Army Douglas MacArthur stated, "The soldier, be he friend or foe, is charged with the protection of the weak and unarmed. It is the very essence and reason of his being ... [a] sacred trust."[20] Moral soldiers do not harm prisoners, and they accept additional risk to safeguard the helpless. As S. L. A. Marshall wrote in the original version of this book, "The barbarian who kills for killing's sake and who scorns the laws of war at any point is repugnant to the instincts of our people, under whatever flag he fights."[21]

The challenge and the moral danger for the soldier who fights under such a code is that in the heat and fury of combat, there are powerful forces, the "forces of moral gravity," which tend to drag the soldier down to the enemy's level. The moral and legal codes that should govern the conduct of American military professionals are those they brought with them to the war, and they must not let themselves be dragged down to the level of an unscrupulous enemy, no matter how strong the temptation. It is particularly the officer's duty to see that service members are not compromised by unworthy actions, even in the heat of battle.

The third category of ethical issues, The Profession and the Society, has two dimensions, both of which have to do with civil-military relations. One is vertical—how the military relates to civilian political leadership. The other is horizontal—how the military relates to the population at large.

The vertical dimension concerns civilian control of the military, a notion firmly established in the U.S. Constitution that gives all the important powers related to the armed forces to civilian officials, in particular to the president as commander in chief and to the Congress to form, organize, and regulate the armed forces in federal service. The actions of both, and those of the Armed Forces, are subject to judicial review by the Supreme Court.

A hierarchy in which political leaders trump military commanders is not unique to the U.S. constitutional setting. As General Sir John Hackett told an Air Force Academy audience, paraphrasing Thomas Hobbes, "Government ... requires an effective military instrument bound to the service of the state in a firm obligation."[22] Subordination of military activities to the needs of government policy was a central concept for Clausewitz, writing almost two hundred years ago in Prussia:

> Subordinating the political point of view to the military would be absurd,
> for it is policy that creates war. Policy is the guiding intelligence and war
> only the instrument, not vice versa. No other possibility exists, then, than to
> subordinate the military point of view to the political.[23]

There is also a horizontal dimension to civil military relations that concerns how the military fits in with the larger civilian society it is sworn to serve.

This zone of values presents a conundrum. For all the reasons given above, the military must maintain a set of values that are critical to its ability to perform the services the state requires of it. Yet, at some times, those very military values might not coexist well with the values of the larger civilian society the armed forces serve. The most salient example is the willing subordination to hierarchy that is the foundation of military discipline, compared to the broad individualism characteristic of the liberal democratic society.[24]

Few theorists or practitioners, military or civilian, hold that the values of the armed forces must always be congruent with those of the larger society. Indeed, there seems to be strong recurrent evidence that members of the larger society harbor an expectation of higher standards of ethical conduct by military professionals than they hold for themselves. Yet, most would argue that when the civil and military values diverge too much, all is not well and dangers lurk for democratic societies. It is not in the interests of either the armed forces or the society for the two to drift apart on important values and attitudes. Members of the armed forces must not disparage the values they have sworn to defend, not least the free expression of views by citizens in free political discourse. Managing this balance is the business of all—military member, political leader, and citizen alike.

The functional and the moral components of the profession of arms elaborated in the last several pages each place enormous demands on the military officer. What integrates them is the concept of the warrior leader. The technical and the ethical dimensions come together in this dual notion of what the armed forces officer must be. The officer must have the fighting spirit, the will to persevere to victory, no matter his or her specialty. "The martial spirit," wrote Morris Janowitz, "continues to give the military profession its distinctive outlook and to mold even its military managers."[25] It remains the unique responsibility of the armed forces officer to ask other people's children to do very dangerous things. These traditions, those of the warrior, must be inculcated, nurtured, and embodied in all officers, so that the armed forces never lose their essential reason for being—the ability to achieve just victory in combat.

Winning in battle is not an individual endeavor: This is a calling that regularly obliges them to order subordinates to kill other human beings. Technical skills and individual proficiency are necessary but not sufficient for the officer to carry out the duties of the office and to earn the "special trust and confidence" that are the basis of the commission. Organizing, mobilizing, motivating, justifying, indeed inspiring others are essential talents for the officer in the profession of arms.

The nature of the warrior leader is driven by the requirements of combat. "War," Clausewitz says, "is the realm of danger; therefore, courage is the soldier's first requirement." But courage, he adds, "is of two kinds: courage in the face of danger, and courage to accept responsibility."[26] The former is physical courage; the latter, moral courage. "The highest kind of courage is a compound of both."[27]

Another way to capture these qualities is to identify the positive character traits of a professional leader we refer to as a leader of character. The demands of war, and even of peacetime service, dictate that the officer must have strength of character—"the ability to keep one's head at times of exceptional stress and violent emotion."[28] This requires, according to Clausewitz, "... first, an intellect that, even in the darkest hour, retains some glimmerings of the inner light which leads to truth; and second, the courage to follow this faint light wherever it may lead."[29] S. L. A. Marshall would agree. "What is the main test of human character?" he asks. "Probably it is this: that a [person] will know how to be patient in the midst of hard circumstance, and can continue to be personally effective while living through whatever discouragements beset him [or her]."[30]

Where stands the profession of arms in the United States in the opening years of the twenty-first century, a time rich in opportunities and challenges? Contemporary American military power and prowess are unprecedented in history, dazzling to friend, foe, and mere observer alike. Technology undreamed of by warriors past is the stuff of everyday life for the American Soldier, Sailor, Airman, Marine, and Coastguardsman. This technology, combined with sophisticated training and grounding in sound moral and legal principles, enables American warriors to fight effectively, while maintaining the highest standards of professional ethics. Americans achieve victory and are expected to do so in the right way. The legitimacy of military action is always subject to public review.

This new century has other challenges. The same technology that yields unparalleled success on the battlefield can also detach the warrior from the traditional ethos of the profession by insulating him or her from many of the human realities of war. Unconsidered, this can blind or desensitize the warrior to the true nature of his or her actions, indeed to war itself. New threats have thrust new missions and new types of combat on our armed forces. Reserve components have been called upon for sustained reinforcement of the active force in duration not seen since the Korean War. They have responded with patience and fortitude at great personal sacrifice. Since 11 September 2001, homeland defense has taken on new meaning and greater urgency. The fighting by Americans may take place not just "over there," but, for the first time since the Civil War, at home as well. Closing with and defeating not just the organized, uniformed armed forces of other nation-states, but the often-elusive combatants of subnational and transnational groups, is the order of the day.

Fighting wars of indefinite duration, with shadowy enemies and ambiguous transition points between war and peace, places additional burdens on the armed forces and on the society they fight to protect. In American military history, victory has usually been difficult and costly, and sometimes elusive, but where lies victory in such a world as this? This century's wars seem to require investment of more effort and blood in building functioning civil societies and ensuring a successful peace than they do in terminating military resistance by conventional foes. The security and prosperity of whole nations are in the hands of our armed forces. Opportunities and challenges abound for the American warrior in the years ahead. These will be exciting, but demanding, years for the officers who lead our armed forces. Selfless service, subordination of individual interests to the wider good, and acknowledgement of the supremacy of civilian government over military requirements will remain defining virtues. The American people will need—and insist on having—the very best men and women to serve as officers. Technically and morally competent officers will have to give their individual and collective best if we are to succeed and prevail over the challenges that face us. We can and we will.

1. General Sir John Winthrop Hackett, *The Profession of Arms* (New York: Macmillan, 1983), 9.
2. Samuel P. Huntington, *The Soldier and the State: The Theory and Politics of Civil-Military Relations* (Cambridge: Belknap Press of Harvard University Press, 1985), 65.
3. Ibid.
4. Carl von Clausewitz, *On War*, edited and translated by Michael Howard and Peter Paret (Princeton: Princeton University Press, 1976), 187.
5. Abraham Lincoln, "Address Delivered at the Dedication of the Cemetery at Gettysburg, 19 November 1863," in *Abraham Lincoln: Great Speeches* (Mineola, NY: Dover Publications, 1991), 104.
6. Hackett, 9.
7. U.S. Department of Defense, *The Armed Forces Officer* (Washington, DC: Government Printing Office 1950), 158. Hereinafter, *The Armed Forces Officer* (1950).
8. "Loyalty: Bear true faith and allegiance to the U.S. Constitution, the Army, your Unit and Other Soldiers" from "The Army Values," FM 22-100 (August 1999), Army Leadership, 2-3.
9. Huntington, 64.
10. Lieutenant General Harold G. Moore and Joseph L. Galloway, *We Were Soldiers Once ... and Young* (New York: Harper Perennial, 1993), xviii.
11. Ibid., 215.
12. James Bond Stockdale, "Ethics Book Dinner, Address to U.S. Naval Academy, class of 1994, 29 March 1994," in *Thoughts of a Philosophical Fighter Pilot* (Stanford: Hoover Institution Press, 1995), 204.
13. Ibid., 203.
14. Morris Janowitz, *The Professional Soldier: A Social and Political Portrait* (New York: Free Press, 1971), 35.
15. Michael Ignatieff, *The Warrior's Honor* (New York: Henry Holt, 1997).
16. Ibid., 116-117.
17. Ibid., 117.

18. Colonel John R. Allen, *Commandant's Intent*, 19 February 2002 version (unpublished document), 3.

19. Michael Walzer, *Just and Unjust Wars*, second edition (New York: Basic Books, 1992), 21.

20. As quoted in ibid., 317.

21. *The Armed Forces Officer* (1950), 15.

22. General Sir John Winthrop Hackett, "The Military in the Service of the State," United States Air Force, *The Harmon Memorial Lectures in Military History, 1959-1987* (Washington, DC: Office of Air Force History, 1988), 509.

23. Clausewitz, 607.

24. Peter Mazlowski, "Army Values and American Values," *Military Review* (April 1990), 10-23.

25. Janowitz, 36.

26. Clausewitz, 101.

27. Ibid.

28. Clausewitz, 105.

29. Ibid., 102.

30. *The Armed Forces Officer* (1950), 16.

CHAPTER 3

MEMBER OF A PROFESSION

There is in armies a tendency to set up an officer group with an otherness, as a step towards, or if necessary ... a replacement of, the betterness you require. The officer is set apart, clothed differently and given distinguishing marks. His greater responsibilities are rewarded with greater privileges. There is some insistence on a show of respect. He is removed from that intimate contact with the men under his command which can throw such a strain upon the relationship of subordinates.[1]

—GENERAL SIR JOHN W. HACKETT

Officers are set apart as a group within the wider profession of arms: in uniform, insignia, responsibility, formal respect required, and limitations on appropriate interaction with other members. In the Armed Forces of the United States, commissioned officers subscribe to a different oath than other ranks. They receive a commission from the president of the United States and serve at his pleasure. The institutional requirement for formal respect is reflected not only in the commission document but in the severity of punishment for offenses against commissioned officers in execution of their office.[2] Indicative of differences in responsibility, there are offenses in the Uniform Code of Military Justice that only an officer can commit, most notably Article 88, "Contempt toward officials," and Article 133, "Conduct unbecoming an officer and a gentleman."

Formal institutional authority and magnitude of responsibility distinguish commissioned officers. The Supreme Court of the United States has observed: "An army is not a deliberative body. It is the executive arm. Its law is that of obedience. No question can be left open as to the right of command in the officer, or the duty of obedience in the soldier."[3] What distinguishes the officer, S. L. A. Marshall wrote, is "exceptional and unremitting responsibility."[4]

In the second chapter, the word profession was used in a general sense to indicate membership in a common vocation. Here it will be necessary to draw finer distinctions. An officer is a professional in two senses: individual and collective. Insisting on the distinction between the two senses is important to give emphasis to the fact of the officer's ultimate individual responsibility to the obligations of the Oath of Office, even when that conflicts with the apparent good of the professional body.

In the individual sense, the officer, like the lawyer, clergyman, or medical doctor, is a specialist, an individual practitioner, employed because of his unique learning, experience, and expertise, to perform a necessary service of value to society. The professional's contribution to society is "the disinterested exercise of professional judgment."[5] The commissioning oath is an individual and highly personal bond with the nation—to well and faithfully discharge the duties of the office—commissioned leadership of the profession of arms.

Officers are first and foremost leaders of Soldiers, Sailors, Airmen, Marines, and Coast Guardsmen. Officers earn the respect of society by success at arms; by faithful service in face of death, injury, and hardship; by living up to the high ethical standards required of those entrusted with the means of war; and by their willingness to direct and care for the men and women in their trust. The individual professional identifies with his or her work and necessarily treats it as a high moral calling. This notion of willing self-identification with the officer's role may not be coincident with commissioning but it marks the point at which the officer truly commits to the notion of being a professional. Until then, he or she remains an apprentice. In this sense, working as a professional involves responding to diverse and highly contextual problems requiring continued delivery of a quality service of a discretionary character. This contrasts sharply with the bureaucrat's routine response by rule to generally similar tasks. Application of an educated discretionary judgment is the real skill of the professional.

This chapter emphasizes a second sense of the concept of a professional, the officer as a member of a profession, part of a self-conscious group of practitioners, pursuing a common calling and practicing under a collective compact with the nation and each other.[6] The nation allows the membership of a profession a high degree of autonomy in recruitment, training, and performance. In return, the profession accepts, collectively, the obligation to assure the competence and ethical conduct of its practitioners, to advance the knowledge of their calling, to train and indoctrinate candidates for membership, and to develop their members throughout their careers.

It is with the military services, organizations established in law, that the government, the constitutional client, establishes the jurisdiction of the profession(s) and the boundaries that govern individual practice.[7] For the officer, "the meaning of meritorious soldiering is determined by the practices and traditions of the professional community he joins."[8] The wide discretion in the performance of professional duties granted the armed forces by the American people, through their elected representatives, underscores the trust placed in the membership to do what is right in all circumstances. When the profession is seen to fall short, the extent of its autonomy is generally reduced, or competitors assume its authority or jurisdiction.[9] For this reason, status as a professional and membership in a profession are both necessary perspectives on the nature of officership. The essence of being an armed forces officer cannot be understood without both concepts.

The notion of the professional officer in the first sense is an old one. George Washington insisted on professional conduct by his subordinates when he commanded a Virginia provincial regiment in the King's service as a young man and later as commander in chief of the Continental army.[10] American reference to the military as a learned profession, similar to medicine, law, or the clergy, can be found in the *Atlantic Magazine* as early as the 1820s.[11] It is possible to see the notion of the professional officer at least as far back as the Roman centurions, long-service men selected for authority. Polybius says:

> Not so much ... the daring or fireeating type, but rather men who are natural leaders and possess a stable and imperturbable temperament, not men who will open the battle and launch attacks, but those who will stand their ground even when worsted or hard-pressed, and will die in defence of their posts.[12]

The specialized knowledge defining the officer changes over time, as do the circumstances in which it must be applied. The content of that knowledge involves the practical and abstract knowledge necessary for disciplined and purposeful direction and leadership of military forces and the management of violence, normally for political ends. Modern armed forces, of course, have many officers who do not engage the enemy directly, or at all. Because the consequences of institutional failure are so devastating to the nation, all armed forces officers subscribe to the warfighting ethic of an indomitable will to succeed, even those whose specialty does not involve direct combat.

Society's respect for the professional officer is conditioned on reliable, ethical, and effective performance of duty. As General William T. Sherman warned officers attending the new School of Application for Infantry and Cavalry at Fort Leavenworth in October 1882:

> No other profession holds out to the worthy so certain a reward for intelligence and fidelity, no people on earth so generously and willingly accord to the soldier the most exalted praise for heroic conduct in action, or for long and faithful service, as do the people of the United States; nor does any other people so overwhelmingly cast away those who fail at the critical moment, or who betray their trusts.[13]

One need look no further than the public outcry to ethical crises at the nation's service academies, or instances when officers are found to have betrayed the public trust or been derelict in their duties, to confirm Sherman's words.

Technical competence in the employment of force or the management of violence is the particular expectation of professional officers. Throughout a career, armed forces officers apply this specialized knowledge and skill creatively to solve unique practical problems, the resolutions of which are of importance to society. This requires development of leadership, as well as more strictly functional skills. In the foreword to the 1960 edition of his book, S. L. A. Marshall wrote of two major roles of the armed forces officer—"as a leader of men, and as a logical, efficient member of the Nation's defense team."[14] The first is predicated on possessing individual skills of human motivation and direction, the ability to influence other men and women to cooperate in a common endeavor, even at risk of life. The second involves individual mastery of the progressively more complex technical and abstract skills of warfighting, as well as in the several departmental functions assigned to the service secretaries and listed in Title 10, U.S. Code—recruiting, organizing, supplying, equipping, training, servicing, mobilizing, demobilizing, administering, and maintaining the nation's armed forces.[15] Most officers will spend a significant part of their professional careers engaged in these strictly departmental functions, which place their own unique demands on the officer's professional expertise.

For the military professional, like medical and legal peers, mastery of a special skill is both the basis of professional authority and the source of a continuing moral imperative. It is the basis of authority because, in exchange for reliable accomplishment in warfighting, society is willing to defer to the military officer's professional expertise on many matters. This acknowledgment of an asymmetry of knowledge and ability between the layman and professional is the basis of the moral imperative for developing and maintaining excellence in technique. Failure to deliver quality in any professional service, be it in the provision of legal advice, medical care, or effective leadership in battle, inflicts a high cost on society. In the armed forces, failure involves the very security of the nation and the lives of the nation's sons and daughters. These sons and daughters are placed in the care and direction of commissioned leaders in trust that their units will enter battle as prepared as humanly possible and that they will be employed in the wisest manner to achieve the nation's purposes at least cost in blood and treasure. Development of the necessary knowledge and skills to live up to this trust requires a lifetime of individual study, training, and long practice by every officer.

The armed forces officer is presumed to have special skills essential to the successful conduct of battle, operations (purposeful sequences of battles), and campaigns. At the junior officer level, these tasks require the teaching skills to train subordinates, the executive skills to set performance standards and to evaluate their achievement, and the leadership skills to direct execution under combat conditions should the unit be committed to battle. A leader must have a fundamental knowledge of human nature and master the technical skills required to employ and maintain all tools assigned, practically as well as conceptually. At higher levels, officers are required to know the weapons and systems found in or available to their units, to organize training and direct employment of subordinate units, and to understand how their roles and missions contribute to the purposes of the whole. They are expected to understand and perform the service functions assigned by law to the service secretaries, even while participating in joint operations. The constant flux in the conditions of professional service, the instruments of combat, and the purposes requiring their employment means that the professional is never free from the need to study and improve his technique or to develop imaginative problem-solving skills. The professional officer must be self-aware, self-reflective, and self-critical to grow personally and professionally.

The traditional notion of the learned profession involved the possibility of a prolonged career.The military career has long since ceased to be a lifetime calling, though it remains a vocation that must be worth one's life. Following the Second World War, to provide a younger force and avoid the promotion freezes that had followed earlier wars, the military services adopted "up or out" selection systems designed to cull the least successful officers at each promotion step allowing for a more pyramidal hierarchical structure for the services. This institutional practice ensures a constant flow of promotion for those who remain and produces a highly competitive system in which everything an officer does weighs in seniors' evaluation of his or her potential for future service as compared to peers.

A level of competition can be healthy for a profession to the extent it inspires individual members to perform at their highest capability. At the same time, competitive selection leads in some cases to egregious careerism and such behavior is sometimes rewarded. Officers must balance their desire for promotion with the needs of their service, their personal ambitions, and, of course, the welfare of their families. It is reasonable for officers to be savvy about the nature of the competition in which they are engaged. Not all postings are equal before selection boards and even the most selfless officer must be aware of the practical requirements of his or her chosen career path. Ethical officers will compete responsibly for the positions that enhance careers and they will keep in mind what the costs of climbing to the top of the tree are not worth.

True professionals give their best effort to whatever task they are assigned and allow the future to take care of itself. The ideal of uniformed service is the collective striving toward a common goal by engaged individuals unencumbered by concerns of individual credit or reward. Those who share hardship and danger develop a rare sense of camaraderie, which often lasts a lifetime and mitigates much of the inconvenience of service. Most officers find the shared nature of military service rewarding. Beyond individual reward or status, they value the engagement with similarly motivated peers, superiors, and subordinates in a common and challenging enterprise of great worth to the nation. Often those individuals with whom one serves become the most instructive teachers and most inspiring role models.

This ideal of collective striving, then, leads to the notion of officers not only as professionals but as members of an honored profession. Whereas professional status is an individual classification based on personal knowledge, abilities, and skills, professions are exclusive, self-conscious, functional collectivities or subcultures entrusted by society to perform or regulate performance of important functions.[16] The Congress charters the armed forces to select, develop, and socialize their members and to certify their leadership. The services operate sophisticated educational institutions to develop new professional knowledge and to train and educate their leaders, particularly officers, progressively throughout their careers. As officers move through basic, intermediate, and senior level education, their professional horizons extend in breadth and depth to prepare them for the next level of institutional responsibility. As professionals, individual officers share the responsibility for their education with the institution and are expected to expand their expertise on the job and on their own through continuous self-study. Members of the profession apply their particular skills individually, according to standards enforced in some way by the group. Armed forces officers protect their status as members of an honored profession by refusing to tolerate practices by fellow members that violate the public trust or norms of the profession.

Professional standards extend beyond simple practice or direction of the common craft to maintenance of a high degree of personal integrity in all dealings, public and private. The enabling legislation of the three principal service departments contains an explicit requirement that: "All commanding officers and others in authority ... are required to show in themselves a good example of virtue, honor, patriotism, and subordination. ..."[17] When members of the profession are seen to fail in their responsibility for self-policing, society withdraws its trust and the profession's autonomy suffers. In addition to maintaining high standards of personal and professional conduct, the American armed forces accept a special public trust in caring for the service members under their charge, first, because the young men and women they lead are the most valuable resource of the nation they serve, and second, because, individually, each service member is or will become a fellow citizen.

Members of the armed forces recognize each other as fellow professionals, according each other, on the basis of their common qualifications and good character, mutual respect and dignity. There are no second-class members in the profession of arms. All the brothers [and sisters] are brave.[18] Officers must be concerned, fair, and just to all service members. Professional officers do not engage in gossip or publicly disparage other officers, other units, and other service members. They must be particularly circumspect and self-disciplined in their treatment and attitude toward members of other races and genders. The armed forces are institutions founded on diversity. Combat readiness depends upon the full participation and contribution of every member, and every member has a right to expect fair and just treatment and reward.

Each service is to some extent a distinct profession framed largely by its unique history and distinct functions. Military action, involving employing forces in or through a particular medium—land, sea, or air—exercises a significant influence, shaping the several service cultures and affecting how the general obligations of military service are observed. The different technical requirements involved in each medium militate against complete unification of the separate services. Still, in the late 1980s, the armed forces began to develop some paraphernalia of a distinct specialist profession for joint service officers, officers drawn from the various commissioning services to serve in joint headquarters and staff. Among these were joint doctrine, joint education facilities, and joint journals dedicated to extending professional knowledge of joint and combined operations. Officers in joint establishments must be able to draw on the individual capabilities of all the services to create innovative synergies, unique and responsive to each particular situation. Thorough knowledge of their parent service is essential, as is the concomitant obligation of their oath and commission to rise above departmental parochialism in service of the whole. This, of course, is equally an obligation of all officers.

Membership in a profession does not mitigate the officer's individual obligations and responsibilities. It does add responsibilities to maintain the standards by which the whole is judged by the client, the American people: to be alert to departures from the norms of professional conduct and to take positive action when they are observed; to participate in the creation and exchange of new knowledge in professional journals and in service and joint doctrine; and to play a role in the training and socialization of the successor generation. It is in the nature of professions that the entire body is often held accountable for the failings of the few.

Legitimate behavior by members of the armed forces acting as a profession is conditioned by the primary individual loyalty of its membership to the Constitution and to the principle of civilian control. On the one hand, the professional is obliged to provide all leaders of government dispassionate expert advice on legitimate matters of professional expertise. On the other, the officer is bound to do so within the limits imposed by the Constitutional position of the president as commander in chief. Just as junior officers are expected to give their full support to seniors' decisions once announced, officers, in the name of the profession, must not intrude on the prerogatives of the commander in chief, nor, simultaneously, on those of the Congress to decide on issues of organization and regulation. That rule holds, even when the decisions made conflict with what officers consider professionally desirable, are contrary to the popular views of the moment, or, often and more painfully, when the leaders of the two branches of government differ and the military member finds him or herself in between. Having rendered their candid expert judgment, professionals are bound by their oath to execute legal civilian decisions as effectively as possible—even those with which they fundamentally disagree—or they must request relief from their duties, or leave the service entirely, either by resignation or retirement. Where this is not possible, the officer must find his or her own moral guidance governing what Robert Bolt's *A Man For All Seasons* called the "little ... little, area ... where I must rule myself."[19] And they must be sure enough and honest enough, to live with the consequences for the rest of their lives.

Professions gained prominence as corporate entities in the last half of the nineteenth century as part of the general process of industrial and societal rationalization. The seminal work on the nature of the American profession of arms is still Samuel Huntington's *The Soldier and the State*, a book written in the mid-twentieth century.[20] As late as the 1980s, Huntington's depiction of the profession as a self-conscious collectivity, carrying out a special type of vocation, characterized by its expertise, responsibility, and corporateness, seemed sound. The American military sustained a sense of corporate identity built around a unique body of knowledge, increasingly specialized and esoteric, not least attributable to the increased complexity of modern warfare. Practical experience and theoretical study in a system of professional schools run by experienced professionals, each with its various research and publishing arms, indoctrinated the leadership with a common way of viewing the military problem. The professions also created new knowledge and abandoned outdated concepts to keep the services in tune with changing requirements of national security.

By the late 1980s, the world was changing with the simultaneous breakdown of the Cold War political order and the breakup of the traditional civil-industrial model and its replacement by a new kind of industrial and professional structure. The coming of instant global communications, the Internet, a general trend to specialization and outsourcing in business, the attendant jettisoning of the notion of lifetime careers, and subordination of those with specialist knowledge to executives whose skills were limited to financial management, marked the rise of postindustrial society. This development carried with it radical changes in the nature of those callings that heretofore had been considered the model professions, none more than the medical profession where the rise of managed health care and increased specialization displaced the independent physician as the professional ideal. Other claimants of professional status also had to adjust.

While this social evolution was under way, the strategic situation of the Cold War, which permitted a national focus on large-scale continental warfare capable of easy extrapolation from the increasingly distant wars of the early twentieth century, experienced its own revolutionary turn. International terrorism and the conditions that spawn it suddenly became the nation's primary concern. Homeland defense and expeditionary warfare introduced new tasks to all armed forces. New means of command and control and new capabilities for precision standoff attack had to be accommodated. Functions, traditionally part of the service repertoire and upon which military success depends, to include armed security and special combat missions, began to be performed in combat zones, on or near the battlefield, by civilians from other government agencies, and by civilian contractors, some of whom were former military members. Today very junior officers find themselves required to influence actions by a variety of civilians not subject to their command and to perform even minor tactical tasks in full view of a judgmental global media. Service cultures and professional identities could not remain unaffected, and the scope of these final changes has raised significant legal, moral, and ethical issues that society, government, and the international community will have to address. All these developments put new stress on the Huntingtonian model of the military profession.

Still, the core task of the profession of arms—to win the nation's battles and campaigns and to sustain the peace—remains unchanged. However the military profession reshapes itself to accommodate the changing conditions of the twenty-first century, certain characteristics are likely to remain constant. Winning the nation's battles and campaigns will remain the central professional preoccupation of all the officers in all the armed forces. The individual obligations of the commissioning oath and the commission are unchanged and are likely to remain so. Commissioned military service, for however long, continues to require a total commitment to serve and a formal and genuine subordination of self to the needs of the nation for the duration of the career. The nation, the members of the profession, and the military institution will continue to demand observation of the values of technical competence, excellence, respect, loyalty, duty, courage, and personal integrity because they remain essential to the accomplishment of the military mission. Officers will continue to be marked by the requirement to maintain and upgrade their special skills throughout their careers. They will be called upon to create new knowledge and new forms of practice as the world around them and the nature of the military problem continues to evolve. They will continue to provide efficient service as members of the defense bureaucracy and effective service as armed professionals. When these two sets of values appear to be in conflict, military professionals will seek balance in the best interests of the nation. Efficiency and effectiveness are not mutually exclusive terms.

In 1980, Herman Wouk reflected on the nature of military service, trying to come to grips with the loss at sea of a Navy pilot he knew who died during a training flight. Wouk captured the timeless essence of professional military service.

> But what did Butch Williams do with his death—this wonderful fighter, this first class man who I believe would have been an important American leader, military and possibly more than military? What did he achieve with this accidental death in routine operations?
>
> I'll tell you what he did—he served. He was there. This man of the highest excellence submerged himself, his life, in this big destructive machine which is our solace and our protection, knowing full well that whether he flew combat missions or routine operations he was at risk. He gave up all the high-priced opportunities in this rich country ... and he served.[21]

---

1. General Sir John Winthrop Hackett, *The Profession of Arms* (New York: Macmillan, 1983), 220.
2. See *Manual for Courts Martial*, Article 90, Assaulting or willfully disobeying superior commissioned officer and compare it to Article 91, Insubordinate conduct toward warrant officer, noncommissioned officer or petty officer.
3. In re Grimley, 137 U.S. 147, 153 (1890), cited as precedent by Chief Justice Rehnquist in *Parker, Warden, et al.* v. *Levy*, 417 U.S., 733 (1974).
4. U. S. Department of Defense. *The Armed Forces Officer* (Washington, DC: Government Printing Office, 1950), 2. Hereinafter, *The Armed Forces Officer* (1950).
5. "A loss of respect," *The Spectator* (17 April 2004), 7.
6. The profession in this sense is a sociological construct developed in the early twentieth century to address work patterns that did not conform to the industrial model. The seminal work on the military profession remains Samuel P. Huntington, *The Soldier and the State: The Theory and Practice of Civil-Military Relations* (Cambridge, MA: Harvard University Press, 1957). Allan R. Millett, a historian at Ohio State's Mershon Center, produced a fairly exhaustive overview of the literature on the concept of a military profession in Allan R. Millett, *Military Professionalism and Officership in America*, Mershon Center Briefing Paper, No. 2 (Columbus, OH: Ohio State University, 1977). See also, Allan R. Millett, "Introduction," *The General: Robert L. Bullard and Officership in the United States Army, 1881-1925* (Westport, CT: Greenwood Press, 1975), 3-15.
7. Title 10, U.S. Code. Implements Congressional authority to raise and support armies and provide for a Navy.
8. Mark J. Osiel, *Obeying Orders: Atrocity, Military Discipline & the Law of War* (New Brunswick, CT: Transaction Publishers, 2002), 17.
9. Andrew Abbott, *The System of Professions: An Essay on the Division of Expert Labor* (Chicago, IL: University of Chicago Press, 1988).

---

10. Don Higginbotham, "Washington and the Colonial Military Tradition," in *George Washington Reconsidered*, Don Higginbotham, ed. (Charlottesville, VA: University Press of Virginia, 2001), 48. See also Glenn A. Phelps, "The Republican General," in ibid., 165-197.

11. "Lectures of Chancellor Kent," *Atlantic Magazine*, 1 (June 1824): 148-149. Chancellor Kent was a legal commentator of the period.

12. Polybius, *The Rise of The Roman Empire*, Ian Scott-Kilvert, trans. (Harmondsworth, UK: Penguin Books, 1979), 322.

13. General William T. Sherman, "Address To The Officers and Soldiers Composing the School of Application at Fort Leavenworth, Kansas, October 25, 1882," available at the Archives, Combined Arms Research Library, U.S. Army Command and General Staff College, Fort Leavenworth, KS.

14. U.S. Department of Defense, "Foreword," *The Armed Forces Officer*, reprint ed. (Washington, DC: Office of Armed Forces Information and Education, 1960), ii.

15. Armed Forces (Title 10), U.S. Code, Sections 3013 (Secretary of the Army), 5013 (Secretary of the Navy), and 8013 (Secretary of the Air Force).

16. A summary of the literature defining the military as a profession in this sense can be found in Millett, *Military Professionalism and Officership in America*, 1977.

17. Title 10, Section 5947 (Navy); Section 3583 (Army); Section 8583 (Air Force).

18. Paraphrase: COL Leonard D. Holder, Commander, 2nd Army Cavalry Regiment, Gulf War (1991), quoted in Michael D. Krause, *The Battle of 73 Easting; 26 February 1991: A Historical Introduction to a Simulation*, Washington, DC: A Joint Project of The Center for Military History and the Defense Advanced Research Projects Agency (18 June 1991), 10.

19. Thomas More in Robert Bolt, *A Man for All Seasons: A Play in Two Acts* (New York: Random House, 1960), 59.

20. Samuel P. Huntington, *The Soldier and the State: The Theory and Practice of Civil-Military Relations* (Cambridge, MA: Harvard University Press, 1957).

21. Herman Wouk, "Sadness and Hope; Some Thoughts on Modern Warfare," *The Naval War College Review* (Winter, 1998–reprinted from September-October, 1980), on-line, Internet, 19 May 2004, available from http://www.nwc.navy.mil/press/Review/1998/winter/art13w98.htm.

CHAPTER 4

DEFENDER OF THE CONSTITUTION AND SERVANT OF THE NATION

By their oaths, members of the armed forces are defenders of the Constitution and servants of the nation. But theirs is a particular kind of Constitution and a unique kind of nation. The Constitution, with its Bill of Rights, is a compact of a self-governing people, providing for a framework of government by consent to complete work begun with an earlier statement of democratic principles, the Declaration of Independence. The Declaration's assertion of unalienable rights established early on the spirit in which the rules of the Constitution would be administered:

> We hold these truths to be self-evident, that all men are created equal, that they are endowed by their Creator with certain unalienable Rights, that among these are Life, Liberty, and the pursuit of Happiness. —That to secure these rights, Governments are instituted among Men, deriving their just powers from the consent of the governed.[1]

The Constitution made implicit the principle of military subordination to civil authority, in recognition of the ultimate source of political sovereignty asserted in the Declaration of Independence. At the same time, it established the spirit that would govern the discipline of the American armed forces. General Washington emphasized military subordination to civil authority in his scrupulous deference to the Continental Congress in his role as military commander. The Declaration of Independence articulated the political expectations of the Soldiers Washington sought to turn into a disciplined regular force to serve the revolutionary effort. Both democratic expectations are as valid today as they were at the beginning of our nation.

In a famous military anecdote, Major General Friedrich Baron von Steuben, the Prussian drill master who transformed the rag-tag Continental army into an organized, disciplined fighting force at Valley Forge, captured an important trait of American Soldiers in a letter to an old European comrade: "In the first place, the genius of this nation is not in the least to be compared with that of Prussians, Austrians, and French. You say to your soldier, 'Do this, and he doeth it'; but I am obliged to say, This is the reason why you ought to do this and that: and then he does it."[2] Like their revolutionary counterparts, today's Soldiers, Sailors, Marines, Coastguardsmen, and Airmen, must understand not only what they must do, but why they must do it. With this in mind, the rest of this chapter explores the concepts behind the phrase, "Defender of the Constitution and Servant of the Nation."

The concept of being a "servant" is uncomfortable to most Americans. The word conjures an image of forced obedience, of slavery, or of menial servitude in contrast to our shared belief in individual freedom. Yet, an officer makes a voluntary choice to serve the nation, to place the nation's interests ahead of his or her personal desires. It is this voluntary commitment that forms the core of the oath of office, the solemn pledge to support and defend the Constitution of the United States. American officers embrace the concept of "service before self."

Officers in the United States armed forces swear to uphold the ideals and obligations embedded in our nation's Constitution, laws, and elected representatives. With the oath of office as an anchor, officers agree to serve the country by fulfilling their duties to the best of their ability and to be loyal, not only to military superiors and branch of service, but to constitutionally elected and empowered leaders and, by implication, to the citizens of our great country. Officers view this concept of service with pride. Instead of menial domestics, they view themselves as "Servants of the Nation," who commit their lives to serve a cause greater than themselves. They must trust willingly the judgment of elected officials and their fellow citizens. In this, officers pledge their abilities, their honor, and, when necessary, their lives. Officers subordinate themselves to civilian control, not as mere servants, but servant-leaders who set the example for their troops. Three historical examples further explain the chapter's concepts: the actions of General George Washington at Newburgh in 1783, General of the Army Douglas MacArthur during the Korean War in 1950-1951, and Major John Key during the Civil War in 1862.

Throughout his command of the Continental Army, Washington exhibited great deference to the position of the Continental Congress. No incident illustrated his stand better, however, than one that came at the end of the war, when victory had been assured. In 1783, two years after the victory at Yorktown, General Washington provided the defining example of a "Servant of the Nation."

As the Continental army began to disband, many officers faced a bleak future. Various states rejected legislation to provide adequate pensions and many officers had lost their property and personal wealth during the long Revolutionary War. These disheartened, disgruntled officers approached General Washington to lead the army to rectify their grievances; in the words of one, to use bayonets "to procure justice to itself."[3] Washington rejected the idea of a military coup in a letter and spoke in a surprise visit to his assembled officers at their final encampment near Newburgh, New York. When his prepared words failed to quiet the gathering, Washington pulled a letter from his pocket to read in one last attempt. He stared at the letter in confusion and anxiety, and then pulled from his pocket something only a few had ever seen him use—a pair of glasses, stating, "Gentlemen, . . . you will permit me to put on my spectacles, for I have not only grown gray but almost blind in the service of my country."[4] This simple act broke the opposition. As old comrades wept, George Washington ended the threat to liberty and the ideals of the Revolution in his closing remarks:

> And let me conjure you, in the name of our common Country, as you value your own sacred honor, as you respect the rights of humanity, and as you regard the Military and National character of America, to express your utmost horror and detestation of the Man who wishes, under any specious pretences, to overturn the liberties of our Country, and who wickedly attempts to open the flood Gates of Civil discord, and deluge our rising Empire in Blood.[5]

In maintaining the subordination of the Army to civilian authority, Washington inspired generations of American officers as the classic example an officer as the "Servant of the Nation."[6]

Somewhat more than a century and a half later, at the end of World War II, General of the Army Douglas MacArthur appeared to most Americans as the ideal "Defender of the Constitution." Renowned for his courageous defense of the Philippines, daring escape from Corregidor, and brilliant "island-hopping" campaign to outmaneuver and outfight the Japanese, MacArthur ranked as the second most popular man in America.[7] Indeed, MacArthur's signature corn cob pipe and crushed, bemedalled service cap created a legendary image, not unlike the heroic image of George Washington. Little did the public expect that within five years, MacArthur would be embroiled in what some scholars called "the gravest and most emotional constitutional crisis" of the twentieth century.[8]

According to John W. Spanier, "The issue at stake was no less than the continuation of civilian supremacy and of the President's authority as Commander in Chief."[9] The Truman-MacArthur controversy shows that defending the Constitution means more than a willingness to risk your life in battle. It also entails that the officer must subordinate personal political, military, strategic, and social views to those of our nation's elected leadership.

Even before the Korean War, General MacArthur challenged President Harry S. Truman's leadership. Following the euphoria of victory in World War II, the nation rode an emotional roller coaster as harsh realities of an emerging Cold

War bucked the nation's psyche. In light of the Iron Curtain, the Berlin crisis, the Communist victory in China, the Soviet explosion of an atomic bomb, and other events demonstrating the end of the wartime alliance, some Americans considered President Roosevelt's successor, Harry S. Truman, a political hack, both unsuited and unqualified for the awesome responsibilities of the office.

In contrast, General Douglas MacArthur's flair, rhetorical skills, and proven battlefield leadership appeared worthy of a great president. MacArthur's benevolent, enlightened rule of occupied Japan further enhanced his presidential appeal. Thus, MacArthur backers placed his name on the 1948 Republican primary ballots in Wisconsin and Nebraska, even while he served in uniform. Although MacArthur was never an official candidate and poor primary showings proved disappointing, the general remained a popular figure and symbol of leadership.[10] The apparent contrast of unequal personalities—the heroic, dazzling MacArthur and the pedestrian, drab Truman—underscored one of the major civil-military crises in American history. Like Washington's behavior at Newburgh, the Truman-MacArthur controversy helps define the concepts of "Defender of the Constitution and Servant of the Nation."

When Communist North Korea launched a sudden, surprisingly effective invasion of South Korea in June 1950, Douglas MacArthur returned to the limelight as a battle leader. Although stung by early, humiliating defeats, American forces rallied, and MacArthur's reputation soared with a spectacular amphibious assault at Inchon that turned the tide of the war.

Buoyed by success, General MacArthur made a series of public remarks critical of the Truman Administration's conduct of the war. In a letter to the Veterans of Foreign Wars, the general, whose strategic responsibilities included affairs in China and Taiwan, repudiated the President's policy to limit war to the Korean peninsula and described government officials as advocating "appeasement and defeatism."[11] Hesitant of rebuking a national hero, the president and Joint Chiefs of Staff (JCS) communicated their displeasure and attempted to restrain MacArthur's policy statements in careful, guarded memoranda and messages. Apparently undeterred, or perhaps unsure of the president's intent, General MacArthur continued harsh criticism of Truman's strategic policies, in particular with regard to the administration's attempt to fight a limited war.

In October 1950, President Truman met with MacArthur at Wake Island to clarify strategic issues and affirm his role as commander in chief. Skeptics thought the unpopular Truman was simply trying to cash in on MacArthur's Inchon success. In their only meeting, MacArthur presented a wide range of strategic issues, apologized for his previous remarks, and assured the president that a United Nations advance into North Korea would not provoke the Communist Chinese into entering the war. After two days of talks, the president and his theater commander departed on good terms. President Truman remarked to reporters, "There was no disagreement between MacArthur and myself. It was a most successful conference."[12]

When a surprise Chinese onslaught smashed American and United Nations troops in November, MacArthur called for drastic measures to defeat the new enemy. Calling for air attacks against China and Manchuria, a naval blockade, the construction of air bases on Formosa, and the addition of Nationalist Chinese troops to Allied forces, MacArthur pressured Truman to widen the war at the same time the president sought to prevent escalation and a possible third world war. Despite the Wake Island meeting and formal guidance from the president and JCS prohibiting unapproved public policy statements, MacArthur sent a strong letter to House Minority Leader Joseph W. Martin denouncing the administration's half-hearted conduct of the war.[13] Representative Martin entered the letter into public debate by reading it to Congress. General MacArthur's text directly violated the president's directives and challenged the administration's policies of restraint with its famous cry that "there is no substitute for victory."[14]

After ineffective attempts to rein in the celebrated general, President Truman relieved MacArthur from command on 11 April 1951, with the full support of his statutory military advisors, the Joint Chiefs of Staff. In his unexpected and unpopular announcement, President Truman stated, "I have, therefore, considered it essential to relieve General MacArthur so that there would be no doubt or confusion as to the real purpose and aim of our policy. . . . General MacArthur is one of our greatest military commanders. But the cause of world peace is more important that any individual."[15]

Although historians debate whether MacArthur intended for Representative Martin to publicize his letter, the distinguished Soldier violated specific orders and the spirit of the commander-in-chief's guidance. MacArthur described his own ideas of what constituted loyalty to the Constitution in a speech to the Massachusetts legislature following his dismissal:

> I find its existence a new and heretofore unknown and dangerous concept, that the member of our armed forces owe primary allegiance or loyalty to those who temporarily exercise the authority of the Executive Branch of the Government rather than to the country and its Constitution which they are sworn to defend. No proposition could be more dangerous.[16]

On the surface, this statement might seem consistent with "supporting and defending" the Constitution, but it is terribly flawed. It presumes to give to the military leader the right or obligation to judge the decisions of his political masters. Officers do not have this right. Wiser words had been offered 50 years before by General John Schofield, who observed before Congress, "Nothing is more absolutely indispensable to a good soldier than perfect subordination and zealous service to him whom the national will may have made the official superior for the time being."[17] Distinguished British military thinker General Sir John Winthrop Hackett points out that MacArthur's concept violates principles basic to any successful democracy:

> That the will of the people is sovereign and no refusal to accept its expression through the institutions specifically established by it—whether in the determination of policies or in the interpretation of the constitution—can be legitimate.[18]

No individual officer, not even a theater commander, possesses the right to determine the legitimacy of the president's positions on national policies. Armed forces officers must serve loyally all elected officials even though those officials might "temporarily exercise the authority of the Executive Branch." The American officer must refrain from individual interpretations of the Constitution. To be a "Defender of the Constitution and Servant of the Nation," officers must promptly and effectively obey the chain of command, regardless of political party or ideological bent. An officer's duty must be to implement state policy and to execute without challenge the lawful orders of elected leadership, reserving advice for legitimate forums and restricting it to matters of professional competence. Officers must not publicly question the effectiveness or validity of national policy.

MacArthur, writes Professor John W. Spanier, "went beyond challenge by appealing over the heads of his civilian and military superiors to the opposition party in Congress and the American people themselves in an attempt to change that policy."[19] This act constituted the heart of a constitutional crisis that stands in striking contrast to Washington's ending of the Newburgh conspiracy.

Washington, of course, was commander in chief of the Continental army at the moment of the nation's birth. MacArthur was a legendary commander who had been chief of staff of the Army 10 years before the Second World War. What does "Defender of the Constitution and Servant of the Nation" mean at less exalted levels of the armed forces? Professor Eliot Cohen tells a story of a Major John J. Key, aide-de-camp to General Henry Halleck in 1862. President Abraham Lincoln cashiered Major Key for saying publicly that the object of military operations against the Confederacy intended no more than to draw out the war to the point where a compromise peace was possible. At the time, General George McClellan, many of his staff officers, and the opposition Democratic Party held these views.

Lincoln dismissed Key, observing: "It is wholly inadmissible for any gentleman holding a military commission from the United States to utter such sentiments as Major Key is within proved to have done."[20] Key's disgrace, which

Lincoln never reversed, was based on the president's belief that Key represented some in the Army who were not fully committed to the defense of the Constitution and restoration of the sovereignty of the national government. By his action the president made clear that total commitment was expected.

By accepting the commission and swearing the Constitutional oath, American officers embrace the concept of civilian control of the military and pledge full loyalty and commitment to the policies of civilian leaders. Officers must strive to be nonpartisan in conduct, speech, and actions, so long as they wear the uniform. Toward the end of his life, MacArthur apparently recognized his previous errors when he reminded West Point cadets:

> Others will debate the controversial issues, national and international, which divide men's minds; but serene, calm, aloof, you stand as the nation's war-guardian, as its lifeguard from the raging tides of international conflict, as its gladiator in the arena of battle. ... Let civilian voices argue the merits or demerits of our processes of government; whether our strength is being sapped by deficit financing, indulged in too long, by federal paternalism grown too mighty, by power groups grown too arrogant, by politics grown too corrupt, by crime grown too rampant, by morals grown too low, by taxes grown too high, by extremists grown too violent; whether our personal liberties are as thorough and complete as they should be. These great national problems are not for your professional participation or military solution.[21]

Although this may be difficult advice to follow in today's world of instant access to global communications and news media, it stands even more important. The American people trust their commissioned officers to carry out lawful orders energetically and implement public policies without hesitation. To be a "Defender of the Constitution and Servant of the Nation" means that you not only protect and obey the laws of our nation, but also the ideals expressed by the Declaration of Independence. American officers must safeguard the public trust in impartial, nonpartisan armed forces through their willing subordination and enthusiastic obedience.

1. "The Declaration of Independence of the Thirteen Colonies," on-line, Internet, 4 April 2004, available from (http://www.law.indiana.edu/uslawdocs/declaration.html).
2. John McAuley Palmer, *General Von Steuben* (New Haven: Yale University Press, 1937), 157.
3. James Thomas Flexner, *Washington: The Indispensable Man* (Boston: Little, Brown, 1974), 171.
4. Ibid., 174.
5. George Washington, "Speech to the Officers of the Army," Headquarters, Newburgh, 13 March 1783, in *George Washington, George Washington: Writings, John H. Rhodehamel*, ed. (New York: Library of America, 1997), 496-499.
6. Flexner, 174.
7. Public opinion polls showed only fellow West Point graduate and former aide to MacArthur, General of the Army Dwight D. Eisenhower, more popular. Burton I. Kaufman, *The Korean Conflict* (Westport, CT: Greenwood Press, 1999), 94.
8. John W. Spanier, *The Truman-MacArthur Controversy and the Korean War* (Cambridge, MA: Belknap Press of Harvard University Press, 1959), vii.
9. Ibid. In fairness, noted historian Professor D. Clayton James argues against the notion of a civil-military crisis and instead focuses on failures of command and communication. See D. Clayton James, "Command Crisis: MacArthur and the Korean War," Harmon Memorial Lectures in Military History, No. 24, United States Air Force Academy, 1982, and D. Clayton James with Anne Sharp Wells, *Refighting the Last War: Command and Crisis in Korea, 1950-1953* (New York: Free Press, 1993).
10. Kaufman, *Korean Conflict*, 94, and Dennis D. Wainstock, *Truman, MacArthur, and the Korean War* (Westport, CT: Greenwood Press, 1999), 9.
11. "General Douglas MacArthur's Letter to the Veterans of Foreign Wars, 17 August 1950," in Kaufman, *Korean Conflict*, 136.
12. Robert H. Ferrell, ed., *Truman in the White House: The Diary of Eben A. Ayers* (Columbia: University of Missouri Press, 1991), 377; quoted in Wainstock, *Truman, MacArthur, and the Korean War*, 69.
13. On 6 December 1950, the President issued two directives: first, all Americans abroad must clear public statements on foreign or military policy through the State Department or Defense Department, respectively; second, all personnel must exercise "extreme caution" in public statements and refrain from direct communication on military or foreign policy with the media. James, *Refighting the Last War*, 204, and James, "Command Crisis," 3.
14. "General Douglas MacArthur's Letter to House Minority Leader Joseph W. Martin, 20 March 1951" in Kaufman, *Korean Conflict*, 150. See also, James, *Refighting the Last War*, 204-208; James, "Command Crisis," 3; Spanier, *Truman-MacArthur*, 4-10; and Kaufman, *Korean Conflict*, 95-96.
15. "Truman's Speech Explaining his Decision to Relieve MacArthur of his Command, 11 April 1951," in Kaufman, *Korean Conflict*, 152.
16. Douglas MacArthur, "War Cannot Be Controlled, It Must Be Abolished," *Vital Speeches* 17 (15 August 1951), 633, quoted in General Sir John Winthrop Hackett, "The Military in Service to the State," Harmon Memorial Lectures in Military History, No. 13 (United States Air Force Academy, CO, 1970), 13.
17. Although little known today, General Schofield served as a Civil War Corps commander, secretary of the Army, and finally Army commanding general. He addressed

these words to Congress following his retirement. Lieutenant General John M. Schofield, quoted in Russell F. Weigley, *Towards An American Army: Military Thought from Washington to Marshall* (Westport, CT: Greenwood Press, 1974, Columbia University Press, 1962), 162.

18. Hackett, "The Military in Service to the State," 13.
19. Spanier, *Truman-MacArthur*, 4.
20. Eliot A. Cohen, *Supreme Command: Soldiers, Statesmen, and Leadership in Wartime* (New York: Free Press, 2002), 39.
21. General of the Army Douglas MacArthur, "Address to the Corps of Cadets Upon Acceptance of the Sylvanus Thayer Award," United States Military Academy, West Point, New York, 12 May 1962.

CHAPTER 5

CHARACTER: NOBILITY OF LIFE AND ACTION

You must know that it is no easy thing for a principle to become a man's own, unless each day he maintain it and hear it maintained, as well as work it out in life.

—EPICTETUS

In February 1943, the troopship *Dorchester* was torpedoed off the coast of Greenland. The Coast Guard Cutter *Escanaba* rushed to the stricken vessel's rescue. The first volunteer swimmer over the side was Ensign Richard A. Arrighi, USCGR. Ensign Arrighi entered the frigid, dark, stormy sea repeatedly, rescuing countless Soldiers and merchant seamen, quitting only when his crude rubber suit became worn and filled with water, and he himself had to be hauled aboard nearly unconscious and treated for exposure. Ensign Arrighi received the Navy and Marine Corps Medal for these heroic efforts in August 1943—posthumously. His ship, *Escanaba*, had exploded two months earlier in the waters between Labrador and Greenland, most likely from a torpedo attack, with the loss of all but two of her crew. Ensign Arrighi's body was never recovered.

The rich collective histories of the armed forces include many similar stories chronicling one Soldier's or Sailor's efforts to save another's life. The unwritten code of "leave no man behind" has driven countless rescue operations, often more harrowing than the original mission itself. Many citations accompanying the Congressional Medal of Honor describe the final chapter in the lives of the brave heroes who perished completing these rescue efforts. This warrior-saving-warrior ethos challenges the armed forces officer to live a noble life worthy of this ultimate measure of dedication.

Previous chapters have articulated a special honor code required of the armed forces officer, which includes standards of conduct far more demanding than other professions. These lofty canons result in a character worthy of America's trust to lead her sons and daughters into harm's way and truly deserving of a comrade's ultimate sacrifice.

What is character? What is its role in the unique challenges and charges of officership? "Leadership," writes General H. Norman Schwarzkopf, "is a potent combination of strategy and character. But if you must be without one, be without strategy."[1] General Schwarzkopf's words affirm that character plays a primary role in defining good leadership. How, then, is character to be defined?

Questions about the existence and development of individual character have a long and complicated history. Ancient philosophers differed in their ideas about the nature of character and did not always agree about the fundamental questions of whether an individual is born with an essential character, or if the choices made in daily life shape one's character. Does character exist apart from the actions that manifest its properties? Aristotelian philosophy reflects a common understanding that character, in essence, has no true value outside of character in practice: "Aristotle constantly reminds his readers that happiness or fulfillment is activity: it is virtue in action, not virtue unused. And virtue as a state of the soul is of value only for the activity which it makes possible."[2]

"Character," according to Aristotle, "is that which reveals choice, shows what sort of thing a man chooses or avoids in circumstances where the choice is not obvious, so those speeches convey no character in which there is nothing whatever which the speaker chooses or avoids."[3] One can realize moral purpose only through the choices one makes; character in theory has limited significance. The choices involved in daily living provide the abstractions with a meaningful shape.

Individuals drawn to careers as officers in the armed forces may enter with similar foundations on which the services can build; these foundations arise from inherent attributes or upbringing. If the American philosopher Ralph Waldo Emerson asserts correctly that "No change in circumstance can repair a defect in character," then the character foundation one brings to the service must have the strength and solidness essential to bear the weight of the responsibility the profession requires from its members.[4] Moral crisis can be avoided if the officer remains in constant and vigilant pursuit of the character ideals that successful military leaders must possess. Associated with excellence in character since ancient times, the Greek concept of Aretè provides useful insights when defining character. The *Oxford Companion to Philosophy* defines Aretè as:

> … excellence, i.e. a quality that the possession of which either constitutes the possessor as or causes it to be, a good instance of its kind. Thus sharpness is an Aretè of a knife, strength an Aretè of a boxer, etc. Since in order to be a good instance of its kind an object normally has to possess several excellences, the term may designate each of those excellences severally or the possession of them all together—overall or total excellence.[5]

The ancient definition of Aretè retains its value today. Just as Homer's Odysseus negotiated the treacherous terrain of his world by relying on character as much as strategy, officers must make the right choices and develop the necessary qualities to face the many temptations to compromise. The armed forces officer can look directly to the core values of each branch of the service to understand the qualities or virtues that all officers must possess to achieve Aretè. Although the virtues vary, common themes emerge, including honor, respect, devotion to duty, service, loyalty, excellence, courage, and integrity. These qualities are like the sharpness of the officer's sword; the officer must develop and maintain them to serve and lead effectively—and to remain worthy of the risks taken by comrades in arms.

Honor: In its simplest and purest form, honor is a compelling moral motivation to do the right thing at the right time. Failure to adhere to one's own sense of honor is the wellspring of guilt and the source of shame. An ancient virtue and the very soul of officership, honor involves a conscious concept of high ethical conduct, moral behavior, honesty, integrity, and trust.

Respect: Respect is the positive regard one person evidences for the shared humanity of another. "[I]n relation to those under his command, [the naval officer] should be the soul of tact, patience, justice, firmness, and charity."[6] Respect is often the least discussed but most important value in leadership. Respect of the leader for the led inevitably earns a corresponding response. Like most concepts of character, respect is often difficult to define; however, it is readily evident when it is observed. Its antithesis, "disrespect," is even more recognizable. Mutual respect is the foundation of teamwork. The best guidance on respect remains the Golden Rule: Treat others as you would have them treat you.

Duty: Duty is a moral obligation to place accomplishment of the assigned task or responsibility before all personal needs and apprehensions. At the extreme end of the spectrum of the tasks assigned are those missions that may require the ultimate level of devotion to duty: to lay down one's life for his or her country.

Service: The officer is the servant of the nation. Service implies subordination and selflessness. Service entails dedicating one's very life to something higher and more important than one's own gratification.

Excellence: Excellence is a deep-seated personal passion for continuous improvement, innovation, and exemplary results in all endeavors. Excellence is fundamental to officership. Unwavering attention to detail and fervor for the extraordinary in every aspect of conduct and performance must be the integral fiber that binds an officer's character.

Courage: Courage is the will to act rightly in the face of physical, personal or professional danger, or adversity. Courage, physical and moral, is inseparably linked to the warrior ethos and the profession of arms. Selfless acts by brave men and women, using their tools and their wits to get the job done under very

45

dangerous, sometimes deadly conditions are the very foundation of the military culture. While bravery, valor, or gallantry under fire are the facets of courage most often associated with the armed forces, officership is more likely to require moral courage than the willingness to face certain death in combat. The fortitude required to consistently do the right thing in spite of personal considerations is far more difficult than dramatic acts of heroism. Admiral James Stockdale, who has reason to know, writes, quoting Epictetus, "Refuse to want to fear, and you start acquiring a constancy of character that makes it impossible for another to do you wrong."[7] Stockdale's words reflect the need to conquer the circumstances that by design or accident threaten to fracture the honor, integrity, and devotion to duty essential to an officer's character and self-respect. Unchallenged maintenance of the lofty core values and concepts recorded on these pages is not effortless; courage is required when risk and personal harm stand in the way.

Commitment: Commitment is total dedication to success. "In whatever we do, we do the very best we can—every single time." This unofficial motto of the Coast Guard captures the effort and focus demanded in an officer's character. From the many extra hours necessary to maintain physical and mental fitness, to the internal fortitude required to overcome what may appear to be insurmountable odds, officership demands unwavering determination, not only to succeed, but to excel!

Loyalty: "Loyalty means a true, willing, and unfailing devotion to a cause. It is closely akin to unselfishness. It entails the complete elimination of our own personal likes and dislikes, hopes, desires, and interests in order that the common cause may triumph."[8] Loyalty is bearing true faith and allegiance to the Constitution. Loyalty is unfailing attachment or steadfastness not only to a cause but also to those who share engagement in its pursuit, subordinates, superiors, and peers. Like respect, loyalty is reciprocal. It is based on mutual trust and regard. Where it is found, it is returned.

Integrity: "Personal integrity also means moral integrity. Regardless of what appears to be some superficial ideas of present-day conduct, fundamentally, today as always, the [individual] who is genuinely respected is the [one] who keeps [his or her] moral integrity sound and is trustworthy in every respect."[9] In 1946, General of the Air Force Henry H. "Hap" Arnold wrote these words in response to a request for advice. The general articulates a timeless and essential truth for every armed forces officer. Of the virtues and qualities drawn from the services' core values, perhaps integrity best captures and summarizes the essence of officership. "Integrity is a character trait. It is willingness to do what is right even when no one is looking. It is the 'moral compass'—the inner voice; the voice of self-control; the basis for the trust imperative in today's military."[10] Integrity refers to holding oneself to a strict moral code in word and deed, a code that forms the foundation for all interaction with subordinates, peers, and superiors alike. It is also the place where the old adage, "lead by example," reaches its zenith. "Walking the talk" is paramount—what one says must completely, identically, and dramatically match what one does. Any sign of hypocrisy will be swiftly, certainly, and harshly judged. The root of the word integrity is the Latin adjective integer, meaning whole. Integrity in a general sense means soundness, completeness, wholeness —all aspects of ones life fit together, complementing one another without contradiction. When what we do matches what we think, how we believe, and what we say, the outcome is an integrated whole—that whole is integrity. Integrity is essential to the core of an officer's character.

These positive values also instruct through opposition. Their negatives reveal the character flaws that officers must never ignore or about which they must never grow complacent. Dishonor, disrespect, apathy, laziness, mediocrity, cowardice, and disloyalty in an officer have an insidious effect on the service and the nation, corrupting purpose and threatening security. Identifying, then mitigating character flaws is an essential and continuous ritual. The armed forces officer serves as a national public figure representing the ethos of heroism in our times. "Service before self" echoes the guiding principle that true strength emerges from the transcendence of individual ego and in the incorporation of the spirit of the whole into one's own character.

The profession of arms demands constant self-awareness, self-reflection, and self-criticism of the times and places when better choices should have been made. Self-awareness plays a crucial role in character development. Former Commandant of the Marine Corps General Charles C. Krulak states, "Sound morals and ethical behavior cannot be established or created in a day … they must be institutionalized within our character over time."[11] By viewing character development as a lifetime pursuit, officers maintain their commitment to Aretè, or total excellence, even when faced with ever-changing environments, challenges, and risks. Chief Justice Earl Warren explained, "The man of character, sensitive to the meaning of what he is doing, will know how to discover the ethical paths in the maze of possible behaviors."[12] The maze may change, but the commitment to the ethical path must remain constant.

If, as Thomas Paine asserts, "Character is much easier kept than recovered,"[13] then it becomes essential for the armed forces officer to remain vigilant against threats to personal integrity. In his letter of instructions to the commanding officers of the revenue cutters, Alexander Hamilton describes the ideal qualities and conduct for officers in contrast with the potential weaknesses:

> While I recommend in the strongest terms to the respective officers, activity, vigilance, and firmness, I feel no less solicitude, that their deportment may be marked with prudence, moderation, and good temper … [a]lways keep in mind that [your] countrymen are free men, and as such, are impatient of

everything that bears the least mark of a domineering spirit ... therefore, refrain, with the most guarded circumspection, from whatever has the semblance of haughtiness, rudeness, or insult ... [e]ndeavor to overcome difficulties, if any are experienced, by a cool and temperate perseverance in ... duty—by address and moderation, rather than by vehemence and violence.[14]

Haughtiness, rudeness, and violence in temperament cannot be tolerated because these flaws in behavior and attitude weaken character.

In classical narrative, a hero has a character flaw, which must be overcome. This struggle for self-mastery drives the plot forward and appeals to readers, who may not possess the same flaw but identify with the universal struggle to master one's weaknesses. In classical drama, the hero often falls because of excessive pride or hubris. Armed forces officers must be vigilant against the weaknesses to which those granted power and public trust become vulnerable. They must guard against feelings of entitlement and privilege. A commanding officer has absolute authority and responsibility for the command and its mission. The enticement to assume entitlement and privilege can easily become overwhelming—especially when one wields the power of life and death.

Demonstrating strength in character may involve making unpopular choices. Concerns about reputation cannot influence an officer's decisions. Faith and moral courage allow an officer to pursue the path most consistent with the core values of the service. According to Roman philosopher Cicero, "Our character is not so much the product of race and heredity as of those circumstances by which nature forms our habits, by which we are nurtured and live."[15]

The spirit of Cicero's words echo in the famous line from Dr. Martin Luther King, Jr.'s "I Have a Dream" speech: "I have a dream that my four little children will one day live in a nation where they will not be judged by the color of their skin, but by the content of their character."[16] The twenty-first-century armed forces officer leads the most diverse crews and units in U.S. history. Men and women of different racial, ethnic, socio-economic, and religious backgrounds join together to serve and desire the opportunity to be judged "by the content of their character." To lead effectively, armed forces officers must strive to understand and embrace diversity. They must strive to incorporate the essential respect into their own character development and root out the assumptions or biases that would impede their leadership capabilities.

The nobility of life that actualizes good character is not always defined by actions that bring renown. When poet William Wordsworth refers to "the best portion of a good man's life,/ His little, nameless, unremembered, acts/ Of kindness and of love," he suggests the goodness or strength in character that one demonstrates through the small acts equal a well-lived life.[17] Through these acts, the spirit nourishes itself and needs no further recognition. These acts remain "nameless" in that no one recognizes them, even the individual who completed them. Through these nameless acts, unmotivated by recognition, the character strengthens in its resolve and becomes better able to face the more formidable tests.

The most formidable evidence of a leader's character comes not from an officer's own actions, but reveals itself through the brave, selfless acts of those Soldiers, Marines, Airmen, Seamen, and Coast Guardsmen they lead: "The true test of a leader is whether his followers will adhere to his cause from their own volition, enduring the most arduous hardships without being forced to do so, and remaining steadfast in the moments of greatest peril" (Xenophon).[18]

At the dedication of the 5th Marine Division Cemetery on Iwo Jima, Chaplain (Rabbi) Roland B. Gittelsohn, USN, spoke these powerful words:

THIS DO WE MEMORIALIZE those who, having ceased living with us, now live within us. Thus do we consecrate ourselves, the living, to carry on the struggle they began. Too much blood has gone into this soil for us to let it lie barren. Too much pain and heartache have fertilized the earth on which we stand. We here solemnly swear: this shall not be in vain. Out of this, and from the suffering and sorrow of those who mourn this, will come— we promise—the birth of a new freedom for the sons of men everywhere. AMEN[19]

To develop one's character diligently and passionately as an armed forces officer involves living a life that respects and redeems perpetually those brave men and women who have served before and who have paid the ultimate price for our freedom and the honor and dignity of your uniform.

---

1. General Norman Schwarzkopf, quoted in *Quotes for the Air Force Logistician*, Beth F. Scott et al., eds., (Maxwell AFB, AL: Air Force Logistics Management Agency, September 2001), 46, on-line, Internet, 29 April 2004, available from http://www. aflma.hq.af.mil/lgj/Quotes%20for%20the%20Air%20Force%20Logistician.pdf.
2. Sarah Broadie, *Ethics with Aristotle* (New York: Oxford University Press, 1991), 57.
3. Aristotle, *Poetics*, on-line, Internet, 29 April 2004, available from Gregory R. Crane, ed., The Perseus Project, http://www.perseus.tufts.edu/cgi-bin/ptext?lookup=Aristot.+Poet.+1450b.
4. Ralph Waldo Emerson, *Essays and English Traits*, vol. 5, The Harvard Classics (New York: Collier, 1909–14), 6, on-line, Internet, 29 April 2004, available from http://www.bartleby.com/5/111.html.
5. Ted Honderich, ed., *The Oxford Companion to Philosophy* (Oxford: Oxford University Press, 1995), 47.

6. John Paul Jones, "Extract from a Letter from John Paul Jones to the Naval Committee of Congress, 14 September 1775," quoted in Augustus C. Buell, "Paul Jones, the Founder of America's Navy: a History," in *Naval Leadership* (Annapolis, MD: United States Naval Institute, 1939), xv.

7. Vice Admiral James B. Stockdale, *Stockdale on Stoicism I: The Stoic Warrior's Triad* (United States Naval Academy, 2001), 18-19.

8. Buell, *Naval Leadership*, 9-10.

9. General H. H. Arnold to Lieutenant Colonel Leroy L. Stephen, 5 Nov 1946, 7 Jan 1947, 2 quoted in Lieutenant Colonel R. Joe Baldwin, "The Leadership Imperative in a Transforming Air Force," *Airpower Journal 7* (Fall 1993): 40; quoted in Captain Mark Williams, "Character and the Core Values of the USAF," Air Force Officer Accessions and Training Schools (unpublished draft), 32.

10. *United States Air Force Core Values* (n. p. : Department of the Air Force, 1997), 1.

11. General Charles Krulak, "Remarks at JSCOPE 2000," 27 January 2000, on-line, Internet, 23 May 2004, available from http://www.geoffmetcalf.com/krulak_20001019.html.

12. Earl Warren, *Christian Science Monitor*, 21 May 1964, quoted in *Simpson Contemporary Quotations*, James B. Simpson, ed. (New York: Houghton Mifflin, 1988), number 1650, on-line, Internet, 23 May 2004, available from http://www.bartleby.com/63/50/1650.html.

13. Thomas Paine, *The American Crisis, no. 13* (April 19, 1783) in *The Columbia World of Quotations*, number 43524, on-line, Internet, April 2004, available from http://www.bartleby.com/66/24/43524.html.

14. Alexander Hamilton, "Letter of Instructions to the Commanding Officers of the Revenue Cutters, 4 June 1791," quoted in *U. S. Coast Guard: America's Maritime Guardian* (Department of Transportation, 2002), 83.

15. Marcus Tullius Cicero, *De Lege Agraria*, II, 95 in *The Columbia World of Quotations*, number 12416, on-line, Internet, 23 May 2004, available from http://www.bartleby.com/66/16/12416.html.

16. Martin Luther King, Jr., "I Have a Dream," Address at Lincoln Memorial during March on Washington 28 August 1963, in *Respectfully Quoted: A Dictionary of Quotations* (1989), number 462, on-line, Internet, 23 May 2004, available from http://www.bartleby.com/73/462.html.

17. William Wordsworth, "Lines Composed a Few Miles Above Tintern Abby, on Revisiting the Banks of the Wye During a Tour, 13 July 1798," in *The Complete Poetical Works* (London: Macmillan, 1888), on-line, Internet, 29 April 2004, available from http://www.bartleby.com/145/ww138.html.

18. Xenophon, *Memorabilia, Oeconomicus, Symposium, Apology*, trans. E.C. Merchant and O. J. Todd Loeb (Cambridge, MA: Harvard University Press, 1923), quoted in *The Military Quotation Book*, James Charlton, ed. (New York: Thomas Dunne Books, 2002), 48.

19. Chaplain (Rabbi) Roland B. Gittlesohn, USN, "The Purest Democracy: Dedication of the 5th Marine Division Cemetery on Iwo Jima, 26 March 1945," U.S. Marine Corps History and Museums Division, on-line, Internet, 23 May 2004, available from: http://hqinet001.hqmc.usmc.mil/HD/Historical/Docs_Speeches/Thepurestdemocracy.htm.

CHAPTER 6

LEADERSHIP

No aspect of an officer's persona and performance is more important than leadership. While leaders exist at all levels within the armed forces, a special burden and a broader scope of leadership fall on those holding a commission. Leadership of other service members is the principal business of officers.

Leadership, according to the Army Leadership Manual, is influencing people—by providing purpose, direction, and motivation—while operating to accomplish the mission and improving the organization.[1] Leadership is not just ordering people around. Troops obey because they must; they follow because they want to. They obey superiors; they follow leaders.

For military leaders, the primary goal is always to accomplish the mission, small or large, tactical or strategic, in peacetime or in war. The requirements of the ultimate mission of war, which is the underlying rationale for the existence of the Armed Forces of the United States ("to provide for the common defense"), set the bar for military leadership quite high. In that bloody crucible, officers must be prepared, competent, and willing to order their troops to take the lives of the enemy and to be ready to give up their lives themselves.

Given the ultimate mission, armed forces officers must build, maintain, and employ warfighting capability. "Creating and sustaining superior fighting power requires the combination of the tangible activities of war—maneuver, firepower, and protection—with the intangible elements of war—leadership, unit esprit, and individual courage."[2] Combining those physical and mental qualities, and molding people into an effective fighting team, requires leadership.

In order to accomplish the mission, whatever it is, the officer must take care of the troops. This is critical both because the officer is legally and morally responsible for their well being and care, and also because if the troops are not well taken care of, it will become difficult, if not impossible, to accomplish the mission. Yet, if the situation requires it, mission accomplishment trumps the welfare and personal safety of subordinates. Mission accomplishment comes first.

Taking care of the troops means attending to their personal needs—physical, mental, and spiritual—and, to a great extent, to their families' needs as well. It also means training and educating the troops for the demands and challenges of their individual jobs and unit missions. In its fullest sense, troop development means going beyond the immediate requirements of the job and the mission to helping them grow in their own careers, preparing them for higher rank, for greater responsibility, and most especially for current and future leadership of their own troops. A good leader leads, and a great leader develops other leaders.

The legendary Commandant of the Marine Corps, General John A. Lejeune, put his own distinctive stamp on the quality of leadership he expected of Marine officers:

> The relationship between officers and enlisted men [and women] should in no sense be that of superior and inferior nor that of master and servant, but rather that of teacher and scholar. In fact, it should partake the nature of the relationship between [parent] and son [or daughter], to the extent that officers, especially commanding officers, are responsible for the physical, mental, and moral welfare, as well as the discipline and military training, of the young men [and women] under their command who are serving the nation in the Marine Corps.[3]

Leadership is a bond of trust. Successful leaders in every field, but especially in the military, all have an ability to gain and maintain the trust and confidence of their superiors, their peers, and their subordinates. In military organizations, leadership is founded on a bond of trust between the leader and the led, trust engendered by the leader's competence, presence, courage, and moral example—and by the military character of the subordinates. "The leader," Sir John Hackett writes, "has something which the others want and which only he can provide. ... A capacity to help people in the overcoming of the difficulty which face them in a joint enterprise. ... The function of leadership cannot be discharged on the one side without a requirement to be led on the other."[4]

Leadership starts with the led, the pride instilled in the individual Airman, Coast Guardsman, Marine, Sailor, or Soldier, pride in who and what they are. Officers must create the bond of trust with subordinates by establishing and maintaining standards, by setting the example, and by being fearless.

Leadership is reflected in unit esprit. It is founded on the pride of the followers, the confidence that they are by virtue of being in military service different and better than the run of the mill, part of something bigger than themselves, something heroic. They must trust that their officers will neither cause them to do anything that would detract from that self-image, nor allow them to fall below the highest standards of duty and performance.

As S. L. A. Marshall wrote, trust is built over time and serves for the long haul:

> While men may be rallied for a short space by someone setting an example of great courage, they can be kept in line under conditions of increasing stress and mounting hardship only when loyalty is based upon a respect which the commander has won by consistently thoughtful regard for the welfare and rights of his men, and a correct measuring of his responsibility to them.[5]

Military subordinates expect their leaders to be competent in their trade. They trust their lives and blood will not be wasted in meaningless actions. "Don't worry, General. We trust you," a 3rd Armored Division soldier told Lieutenant General Fred Franks, the VII Corps Commander, on the eve of the ground attack in Operation *Desert Storm*.[6] "Marines," according to the Marine Corps leadership manual, *Leading Marines*, "have a reasonable expectation that their leaders will come up with plans that will accomplish the mission and give them the best possible chance of succeeding. They do not ask for certainty, just the best possible preparation and skills from their leaders."[7] Leaders, in turn, trust their subordinates to respond to direction with alacrity and to perform in accordance with the high standards of their service.

Trust is a two-way street, a mutual relationship between leaders and those they lead. A leader builds and nurtures trust in an organization both by being trustworthy and by being trusting. Troops must be able to take the leader's word at face value and have full confidence in his or her technical competence and moral character. But the second face of trust is equally essential: troops must know that their leaders have confidence in them and take their word at face value. The officer who continually second-guesses the troops or micro-manages them will not be leading an organization distinguished by trust, and thus that officer will fail in a primary obligation. As Admiral William Crowe put it when he was Chairman of the Joint Chiefs of Staff, "You cannot run a unit just by giving orders and having the Uniform Code of Military Justice behind you."[8]

Leaders are expected both to interpret the orders of higher authority, translating them into meaningful tasks for accomplishment by their subordinates, and to buffer the troops from the storms that originate above. This latter can be easily misunderstood. Officers are not shop stewards. "Officers occupy the middle ground."[9] Their function is to get the most out of the unit for which they are responsible, while protecting their charges from unnecessary burdens, but they understand that the final determination of what is necessary will not be made by them. General Powell describes the expectations of Soldiers for their lieutenant:

They will look to you for inspiration, for a sense of purpose. They want to follow you, not be your buddy or your equal. You are their leader. They want someone in charge who they can trust—trust with their lives. They want someone they respect, someone they can be proud of. They want to be able to brag about their lieutenant.[10]

Officers do not shirk their responsibilities. Orders they give are their orders, not those of some higher authority. In the same vein, the responsibility is theirs, and they do not pass it on. Troops get the credit. Officers accept the blame. When an order appears to make no sense, subordinates expect it will be questioned and better alternatives offered if available. Superiors expect that the order will be executed with energy if it stands.

Leaders keep everyone focused on the mission and on winning. According to General Colin Powell, the troops "expect you to lead them to win, whether in battle or peacekeeping, to accomplish the mission given by the Nation."[11]

Leaders set and enforce the standards. New officers often do not understand that failing to set high standards, and more important, failing to respond with disapproval when they are not met, undermines their authority. Lax standards are not what the troops need, want, and have a right to expect. John Baynes, a retired British infantry officer, has observed:

> A strictly imposed discipline is not condescending. ... To allow a soldier to disobey orders is really to insult him. A good man, in any walk of life, knows what he can do, and what he should do. If he fails, he expects the just reward of failure. ... A man in authority who lets his subordinates get away with poor performance implies in doing so that they and their actions are of no significance. ... Tolerance is not only disliked by the soldier for its implications that his efforts do not matter much, but also because it is to some extent an abnegation of duty by his superior.[12]

S. L. A. Marshall put it more simply: "The level of discipline is in large part what the officers in any unit choose to make it. ...To state what is required is only the beginning; to require what has been stated is the positive end."[13]

An American exemplar of military leadership (and of much else as well), General George Washington, gave this advice on discipline:

> ... be strict in your discipline; that is, to require nothing unreasonable of your officers and men, but see that whatever is required be punctually complied with. Reward and punish every man according to his merit, without partiality or prejudice; hear his complaints; if it is well founded, redress them; if

otherwise, discourage them, in order to prevent frivolous ones. Discourage vice in every shape, and impress upon the mind of every man, from the lowest to the highest, the importance of the cause, and what it is they are contending for.[14]

Setting and maintaining standards involve learning "what right looks like," demonstrating it by personal example, and being satisfied with nothing less from everyone in the unit, officers and enlisted alike. The Marines say, "Whenever two Marines are together ... one is in charge," meaning that the "senior Marine present" is responsible for ensuring that both of them adhere to the standards of the Corps.[15] In a similar vein, "Every soldier is a leader, responsible for what happens in his or her presence regardless of rank."[16] Leaders must accept responsibility and accountability for everything that happens in their unit, even when they are not physically present. By setting demanding, but achievable, standards leaders develop sound and proud units.

Leaders set the example. Commissioned leaders earn their authority by setting the example in their conduct both on-duty and off-duty. Officers are expected to model high moral standards, reflecting virtue, honor, patriotism, and subordination of self. *Leading Marines* puts it succinctly:

> Commanders will impress upon all subordinate officers the fact that the presumption of integrity, good manners, sound judgment, and discretion, which is the basis for the special trust and confidence reposed in each officer, is jeopardized by the slightest transgression on the part of any member of the officer corps. Any offense, however minor, will be dealt with promptly, and with sufficient severity to impress on the officer at fault, and on the officer corps.[17]

In fact, there are four aspects of military performance in which even the greenest officer can set the example for more experienced troops: discipline, military bearing, appearance, and physical fitness. Discipline begins with self-discipline: "No man is fit to command, who cannot command himself."[18] Military bearing requires little more than carrying oneself confidently and speaking in a clear and forthright manner. The uniform should fit properly and be worn correctly, because what the officer does, immediately becomes the standard for the troops to follow. Physical fitness is essential to proper performance of duty in any service. It provides for stamina, particularly in periods of stress. The new officer may have much to learn about how to operate complex military equipment, or direct tactical maneuvers under stress, but there is no reason he or she cannot fall-in for physical training and set a standard for subordinates to emulate.

To be effective, the new officer must master the techniques involved in the work of subordinates. He or she must be willing to ask intelligent questions and to learn quickly. In time, S. L. A. Marshall wrote, the ability "to do the work of any man serving under him ... so that his men begin to understand that he is thoroughly versed in the work problems that concern them ... is the real bedrock of command capacity."[19] Here, the time-honored practice of "management by walking around" can be quite helpful to the officer.

Leaders model courage, physical and moral. Combat is the domain of danger and uncertainty, in which physical courage and moral courage are challenged on all sides. Sir John Hackett says the requirements for an officer at war are bravery, competence, tirelessness, and calm.[20] Along the same lines, S. L. A. Marshall identifies courage, creative intelligence, and physical fitness.[21]

Physical courage in a leader is most often expressed in a willingness to act, even alone if necessary, in situations of danger and uncertainty. Marshall observes:

> Among the commonest of experiences in war is to witness troops doing nothing, or worse, doing the wrong thing, without one commanding voice being raised to give them direction. In such circumstances, any man who has the nerve and presence to step forward and give them an intelligent order in a manner indicating that he expects to be obeyed, will be accepted as a leader and will be given their support."[22]

To give that order, the officer must be present: It is difficult, if not impossible, to lead from the rear. Here, too, the officer leads by example, and when it is most needed, that example can be inspiring. Leaders are obligated to overcome the natural fear, which afflicts them as well as their subordinates, and to continue to function and to lead, even in the face of great personal danger. That is what physical courage is all about.

Leaders can prepare themselves and those they follow for moments of stress and danger by anticipating what they are likely to face and preparing themselves mentally to respond instinctively. Battle drills for small units, battle station drills on ships of war, and practice emergency procedures for aircrew are intended to hone instinctive and effective response to threats. As shown in Chapter 1, Lieutenant Commander John Waldron had prepared his unit and himself mentally for the deadly torpedo run at Midway.

Moral courage is different from physical courage, but it is just as necessary, and the demands it places on the officer are just as formidable. "The highest kind of courage is a compound of both."[23] Simply put, moral courage is the courage to do what is right, even when it is difficult or not in your immediate best interests.

In war, where they might be horribly injured or even killed, officers bear the moral burden of ordering men and women they lead to perform tasks that would ordinarily be censured by society: to take others' lives. It requires enormous moral strength to bear the burden of command for prolonged periods when one's subordinates are wounded and killed, frequently because of decisions the officer makes under pressure of events.

Simultaneously with bearing the burden of ordering actions directly destructive of life and limb, the officer is responsible for protecting troops from the dehumanizing effects of the nature of what they do and from the moral perils their jobs might seem to involve. "Marines don't do that," a Marine lieutenant is said to have told a subordinate getting ready to destroy a Vietnamese farmer's hut without cause. Taking care of the troops is professional and moral bedrock for the military, and officers who place their troops in moral or legal jeopardy are not taking care of them. The officer who does so violates something deeply imbedded in the DNA of the military profession.

In wartime, and under stress, all eyes turn to the leader: "What do we do now, Lieutenant?" The physical and moral courage, the values, and the confidence the officer retains in face of every trial are often what get the unit through their shared ordeal.

The need for moral courage is not confined to the battlefield. If the troops see their officer cutting corners, evading responsibility, lying, or even shading the truth, in order to accomplish some goal, they will draw their own lessons about what is acceptable behavior and what is not. Every decision an officer makes, and every action he or she undertakes, becomes, wittingly or not, a potential precedent or model for the future behavior of the troops. They will pay as much attention, and perhaps even more, to what the officer does as to what the officer says.

Leaders build and sustain morale. Leadership, by its very nature, is not a solitary activity, no matter how lonely it may feel at times. It always involves others, individually and as a unit. In his memoir of service with the British Army in the Middle East and Burma, John Masters relates a speech Field Marshall "Bill" Slim gave early in the war on the subject of morale:

> In the end every important battle develops to a point where there is no real control by senior commanders. Each soldier feels himself to be alone. Discipline may have got him to the place where he is, and discipline may hold him there—for a time. Co-operation with other men in the same situation can help him to move forward. Self-preservation will make him defend himself to the death, if there is no other way. But what makes him go on, alone, determined to break the will of the enemy opposite him is morale. Pride in himself as an independent thinking man, who knows why he's there,

and what he's doing. Absolute confidence that the best has been done for him, and that his fate is now in his own hands. The dominant feeling of the battlefield is loneliness, gentlemen, and morale, only morale, individual morale as a foundation under training and discipline will bring victory.[24]

The collective equivalent of morale is unit esprit—a palpable sense of being part of something larger, something better, and the bonds that tie the individual unit members into a cohesive whole. The Marines again capture it well: "Esprit de corps, then, depends on good leadership primarily, but there are other factors. The term implies not only respect between officers and enlisted ... but also a feeling of confidence and comradeship among Marines themselves."[25] Esprit is the mental and emotional state of the entire unit, which then motivates the members to overcome what are at times seemingly insurmountable obstacles, to be willing to suffer, even to die, for each other.

To return to the theme with which the chapter began, S. L. A. Marshall said of esprit, it "is the product of a thriving mutual confidence between the leader and the led, founded on the faith that together they possess a superior quality and capability."[26] Leaders recognize the esprit in units, even in peacetime, by the pride they take in the little visible things like wear of the uniform, the sharp salute, a bit of swagger, and meticulous attention to detail. The snap of the guard at the gate speaks volumes of the heart of the organization.

The opportunities and types of leadership differ among, and within, the armed forces according to the nature of their combat roles. For example, Army and Marine ground combat leaders, even as very junior officers, practice a very direct kind of leadership with large groups of enlisted personnel. In contrast, Air Force, Marine, and Navy pilots seldom get to practice unit leadership on a similar scale until they reach the middle grades of their profession. On the other hand, as a pilot, a junior officer may command a crew that includes more senior officers. Junior Coast Guard officers commanding isolated stations exercise an extraordinary degree of initiative. Division heads on ships practice a style of leadership unique to the sea services in its formality. Each example requires different, but equally important, leadership skills. Commissioned leaders depend upon the experience and maturity of noncommissioned deputies to complement their own knowledge and to support their authority and responsibility.

Despite occasional references to someone as "a born leader," leadership in fact is an acquired skill, something learned, "an art mainly acquired by observation, experience, and emulation."[27] Leadership is as much a matter of the heart and soul as of knowledge. There is no simple formula that will guide all new commissioned leaders to complete success. *Leading Marines* lists 11 requirements for leaders that are useful for officers of all services, of all pay grades, in all military occupational specialties:

- Be technically and tactically proficient
- Know yourself and seek self-improvement
- Know your Marines and look out for their welfare
- Keep your Marines informed
- Set the example
- Ensure the task is understood, supervised, and accomplished
- Train your Marines as a team
- Make sound and timely decisions
- Develop a sense of responsibility among your subordinates
- Employ your unit in accordance with its capabilities
- Seek responsibility, and take responsibility for your actions.[28]

---

1. Department of the Army, *Leadership*, FM 22-100 (31 August 1999), 1-4.
2. *Leading Marines* FMFM 1-0 (Washington, DC: Department of the Navy, Headquarters, U.S. Marine Corps, 1995), 81.
3. Ibid., 97.
4. General Sir John Winthrop Hackett, *The Profession of Arms* (New York: Macmillan, 1983), 216.
5. U.S. Department of Defense, *The Armed Forces Officer* (Washington, DC: Government Printing Office, 1950), 161. Hereinafter, *The Armed Forces Officer* (1950).
6. General Frederick M. Franks Jr., "Battle Command: A Commander's Perspective," *Military Review*, Vol. LXXVI, No. 3 (May-June 1996), 4.
7. *Leading Marines*, MCWP 6-11 (Washington, DC: Department of the Navy, Headquarters, U.S. Marine Corps, November 2002), 87.
8. *Newsweek*, April 18, 1988, as found in Peter G. Tsouras, *Warriors Words – A Quotation Book* (Arms and Armor Press, 1992), 302.
9. This formulation was shared with some of the authors of this book by VADM Rodney Rempt, Superintendent of the U.S. Naval Academy, in September 2003 at the McCain Conference, an annual all-service academy meeting organized by the Center for the Study of Professional Military Ethics.
10. General Colin Powell, "1998 Sylvanus Thayer Award Speech," Assembly (November/December 1998), 79.
11. Powell, 79.
12. John Baynes, *Morale: A Study of Men and Courage* (Garden Park, NY: Avery, 1988), 186-187.
13. *The Armed Forces Officer* (1950), 141.
14. Letter to William Woodford, 10 November 1775, *The Writings of George Washington*, Vol. 4, 1931-1944, as found in Tsouras, *Warrior Words*, 139.
15. *Leading Marines*, 33
16. Les Brownlee and Peter J. Schoomaker, "Serving the Nation at War: A Campaign Quality Army with Joint and Expeditionary Capabilities," *Parameters*, XXXIV, No. 2 (Summer 2004), 13.
17. Quoted in *Leading Marines*, 94.

---

18. Colonel Robert D. Heinl, Jr., USMC (Ret.), *Dictionary of Military and Naval Quotations* (Annapolis, MD: Naval Institute Press, 1966), 59.
19. *The Armed Forces Officer* (1950), 170.
20. Sir John Hackett, *The Profession of Arms* (New York: Macmillan, 1983), 216.
21. *The Armed Forces Officer* (1950), 82.
22. *The Armed Forces Officer* (1950), 111.
23. Carl von Clausewitz, *On War*, edited and translated by Michael Howard and Peter Paret (Princeton: Princeton University Press, 1976), 101.
24. Field Marshall Sir William "Bill" Slim quoted in *John Masters, The Road Past Mandalay; A Personal Narrative* (New York: Bantam Books, 1979), 39-40
25. *Leading Marines*, 49.
26. *The Armed Forces Officer* (1950), 160.
27. Colonel Robert D. Heinl, Jr., USMC (Ret.), *The Marine Officers Guide*, 4th edition (Annapolis, MD: Naval Institute Press, 1977), 367.
28. *Leading Marines*, 91.

CHAPTER 7

RESPONSIBILITY, ACCOUNTABILITY, AND DISCIPLINE

The essential basis of the military life is the ordered application of force under an unlimited liability. It is the unlimited liability which sets the man who embraces this life somewhat apart. He will (or should be) a citizen. So long as he serves he will never be a civilian.[1]

—GENERAL SIR JOHN W. HACKETT

Responsibility, accountability, and discipline are three independent, yet interrelated, core concepts of the military profession that separate you from your civilian contemporaries. Responsibility involves acknowledging your duties and acting accordingly. Accountability means "the buck stops here," neither shifting blame to others nor taking credit for others' work or success. Discipline entails following orderly, prescribed conduct, and punishing those who fail to meet their responsibilities or established standards.

In the 1950 edition of *The Armed Forces Officer*, S. L. A. Marshall notes the deference a nation gives to military officers because of the responsibility they accept when commissioned:

> They accept the principle that some unusual advantage should attend the exceptional and unremitting responsibility. Whatever path an American officer may walk, the officer enjoys prestige. Though little is known of the officer's intrinsic merit, the officer will be given the respect of fellow citizens, unless that officer proves to be utterly undeserving.[2]

Responsibility, accountability, and discipline. These three common terms have spawned numerous interpretations and debates over the years. However, across the divergences, some important common truths become apparent.

Responsibility. General Curtis E. LeMay was once asked to provide a one-word definition of leadership. After some thought, he replied, "Responsibility." As a military officer, you voluntarily commit to the associated duties and obligations of your commissioning oath: "I take this obligation freely without any mental reservation or purpose of evasion." You maintain this responsibility to duties and obligations and to performing your unit's mission until you leave the service.

Accountability. The *Merriam-Webster Dictionary* defines accountability as "an obligation or willingness to accept responsibility or to account for one's actions" and lists responsible as a synonym for accountable.[3] If you fail to uphold your responsibilities (i.e., perform your unit's mission), you are accountable for the consequences and face appropriate disciplinary action if appropriate. In short, accountability prevents carelessness. Otherwise we could feel free to make irresponsible decisions or forget to carry out our duties, unnecessarily [endangering] the safety of our [people or our resources].[4]

Discipline. In a July 1759 Letter of Instructions to the captains of the Virginia Regiment, which he commanded, George Washington observed, "Discipline is the soul of an [a]rmy. It makes small numbers formidable, procures success to the weak, and esteem to all."[5] A decade and a half later, after one look at the mob that the Continental Congress called an army, General Washington insisted that the Founding Fathers establish a system for meting out punishment. In response to his demands, Congress borrowed the English Articles of War and gave the commanding general a formalized system of military justice. Washington recognized that discipline, enforced by an even-handed system and credible administration of justice, is the backbone of an effective fighting force.[6]

Although responsibility, accountability, and discipline have only been discussed in simplistic terms thus far, consider how each factors into the following examples.

At 0210, 4 December 1989, a U.S. Coast Guard cutter went aground off Keweenaw Point in Lake Superior after completing buoy operations. It ultimately sank, after its entire crew was forced to abandon ship. Fortunately, no lives were lost but the World War II-era ship, valued at approximately $29 million, was. What precipitated the grounding? At 0202, just several minutes prior to the grounding, the commanding officer left the bridge for his stateroom and the mess deck without looking at the chart of the area or verifying the vessel's position. The officer of the deck also failed to verify the ship's position in accordance with the commanding officer's standing orders and made wrong assumptions about the commanding officer's approval of the ship's track. The board of investigation concluded that the proximate cause of the grounding was the failure of the officer of the deck and commanding officer to properly carry out and supervise the required standard practices of navigation in accordance with Coast Guard regulations and the commanding officer's own standing orders, while maneuvering at night and in unfamiliar, restricted waters.[7]

The commanding officer was issued a letter of reprimand for "his dereliction of duty and his negligence in the safe navigation of his vessel that resulted in the stranding and subsequent loss of his vessel." The officer of the deck received a letter of reprimand for "her dereliction of duty and her failure to obey a lawful order as expressed in the Commanding Officer's Night Orders."[8]

In regards to responsibility, both the commanding officer and the officer of the deck were responsible for the safe operation of the vessel. How? The commanding officer was responsible for ensuring proper procedures were established to ensure safe operations, while the officer of the deck was responsible for ensuring those safe operations were carried out. Both individuals failed to uphold this responsibility, were held accountable for their actions, and subsequently disciplined in the form of punitive action for their failures.

On 9 February 2001, USS *Greeneville* was operating south of Oahu, Hawaii, conducting a seven-hour Distinguished Visitor Cruise. At approximately 1300 the executive officer informed the commanding officer that the ship needed to start afternoon ship demonstrations, including an emergency surfacing maneuver, for the civilian guests. At that particular time, *Greeneville* was 12-13 miles away from its next scheduled point of location and more than 30 minutes behind the schedule posted in the Plan of the Day.[9] As it rose to the surface, *Greeneville* collided with Japanese motor vessel *Ehime Maru*, a "moving classroom" for high school students preparing for employment in the marine products industry. *Ehime Maru* sank in less than 10 minutes; of 35 Japanese crew, instructors, and students on board, 26 were rescued—the remaining nine members died.[10]

A subsequent Naval Court of Inquiry's report of investigation determined there were two fundamental causes for the collision: (1) *Greeneville* completed only an abbreviated sonar and periscope search that did not conform to standard operating procedures or the commanding officer's own standing orders, and (2) the ship's watch team failed to work together and pass information to each other about the surface contact picture.

> The reason for these two causes is quite clear. The Commanding Officer, USS Greeneville created an artificial sense of urgency in preparation for surfacing on 9 February when prudent seamanship, the safety of his submarine and good judgment dictated otherwise. In doing so, he marginalized key contact management and Control Room personnel, cut corners on prescribed operational procedures, and inhibited the proper development of the contact picture.[11]

In a Memorandum for the Record, dated 23 April 2001, Commander in Chief of the U.S. Pacific Fleet Admiral Thomas Fargo issued the following statements:

> Commander X's disregard of his own standing orders and guidance provided by Naval Warfare Publications was a cause of the collision... operational standards on board USS Greeneville, starting with the Commanding Officer and permeating throughout the crew, were relaxed and casual. [Additionally] ... the collision was caused by Commander X's perceived desire to hurry the evolutions in the afternoon to prevent a late arrival at the entrance to Pearl Harbor.[12]

The commanding officer was ordered to Admiral's Mast and was found to have violated Article 92, Uniform Code of Military Justice (UCMJ) (Dereliction in the Performance of Duties) and Article 110, UCMJ (Negligent Hazarding of a Vessel). He was issued a punitive letter of reprimand, forfeited one-half of his pay for two months (with forfeitures suspended for six months), and removed "for cause" from his previous duties as commanding officer, USS *Greeneville*, actions which effectively terminated his career.[13]

These cases clearly depict the relationship among responsibility, account-ability, and discipline. Additionally, they highlight the critical point that respon-sibility and accountability are applicable not only in combat situations. In fact, most of your challenges in these arenas will develop during routine, day-to-day operations such as the Coast Guard or Navy incidents. Finally, the USS *Greeneville* incident clearly reveals how miscues can lead to tremendous loss of life and resources, both domestically and on the international front. A more in-depth look at responsibility, accountability, and discipline, with accompanying case studies, will better define the respective role each of these concepts plays in your career.

Responsibility. Following the disastrous third day's attack at Gettysburg, in a battlefield dialog with Major General Cadmus M. Wilcox, General Robert E. Lee fully personified the concept of responsibility: "Never mind General," he told his shaken subordinate, "all this has been my fault; it is I that have lost this fight, and you must help me out of it."[14] As both Lee's comment and the Coast Guard cutter case study illustrate, the demands on you as a military officer are great, and the weight of this responsibility is individual and compounds with rank and position. This professional and moral responsibility is a total commitment. It runs the entire gamut—from maintaining standards of dress and appearance, to observation of customs and courtesies, to maintenance of proper human relations and professional relationships, to the utmost challenge—giving orders to your Airmen, Sailors, Soldiers, Coast Guardsmen, or Marines to kill other human beings or to risk being killed themselves. No other single profession demands this constant, far-reaching level of responsibility of its members, regardless of rank or rate.

One of the unique distinctions of the officer profession is that you are responsible for all the personnel, equipment, and missions that you lead—24 hours a day, seven days a week. Furthermore, you are responsible for your subordinates' actions, even for an outcome you did not directly cause, as illustrated in the following case study involving a Marine lieutenant serving as a rifle company commander at Twenty-nine Palms, California.

During a 1992 training exercise, a Marine lance corporal was posted as a road guide during night maneuvers in the Mojave Desert, 200 yards away from his partner—in violation of standard procedure but by the order of his lieutenant. When the maneuvers ended, the lance corporal was overlooked by a truck convoy and accidentally left behind in the desert. The lieutenant's subordinate, a Marine gunnery sergeant, was charged with accounting for all the Marines and erroneously reported 100 percent accountability. After nearly two days, the lance corporal was reported missing and a search ensued. Tragically, the lance corporal's body was found, several hundred yards from where he was last seen; the desert heat was apparently responsible for his death. An investigation ensued and dereliction of duty charges were filed against the lieutenant. The court-martial panel held the lieutenant responsible for the lance corporal's death, convicted him, and sentenced him to four months in the brig and dismissal from the Marine Corps.[15]

Why did the lieutenant pay the price for the death of the Marine, when he had assigned the responsibility of ensuring all were present to the gunnery sergeant? In assigning responsibility, the lieutenant did not relinquish his ultimate responsibility and accountability for the welfare of his troops. The gunnery sergeant was given the authority to act on behalf of the lieutenant and to share the responsibility. Delegation of authority never absolves you, the officer, of your inherent responsibility to see that obligations are met, even when accomplished by subordinates. You have absolute responsibility for everything and everyone under your care, particularly the safety and well being of your people.[16] You cannot delegate responsibility. Your duty and obligation is to the mission of the unit. If anything under that command falls short, you are accountable for the shortcoming, regardless of its cause. The lieutenant was held accountable for the tragedy and paid the price for the failure of his subordinate to execute a duty. Succinctly put, being "held responsible" is synonymous with being "held accountable."

Along with responsibility must go accountability. Without accountability, having to answer for what one has not done, either good or bad, one has no responsibilities. If an officer has no responsibilities for which he or she will be held accountable, followers will find it difficult, if not impossible, to place their confidence and trust in that leader.[17]

Accountability. In an August 1995 video message, Air Force Chief of Staff Ronald Fogleman gave his views on Air Force standards and accountability. General Fogelman's words on accountability apply to all service members everywhere:

> The principle that good order and discipline are essential to combat effectiveness has not changed throughout the years. Good order and discipline. At the very foundation of those concepts must be standards that are uniformly known, consistently applied, and nonselectively enforced. Our military standards are higher than those in our society at large because of what we do. We defend our nation. The tools of our trade are lethal. We are held to a higher standard by the public and we are held in high regard by the public because of the integrity we demonstrate by holding ourselves accountable and others accountable for their actions. ... [F]ailure to ensure accountability will destroy the trust of the American public—the very people living under the Constitution we swore to support and defend, and who look to us, the members of their nation's Air Force, to embrace and live by the standards that are higher than those in the society we serve."[18]

The tape was made following the 14 April 1994 Black Hawk incident when two F-15Cs of the 53d Fighter Squadron, enforcing the "no fly" zone over northern Iraq, mistakenly shot down two Army Black Hawk helicopters engaged in United Nations humanitarian missions for the Kurds, killing all 26 passengers: 15 Americans, five Kurdish civilians, and British, French, and Turkish military officers. Investigations by the Air Force resulted in charges of dereliction of duty against a crew member, an Air Force captain, of the Airborne Warning and Control System (AWACS) aircraft controlling the airspace at the time, and charges of negligent homicide and dereliction of duty against one of the F-15 pilots and four other AWACS crew members. The AWACS captain was acquitted and charges against the others were dropped following Article 32 investigations. Altogether, eight officers were reprimanded, counseled, or admonished, and one was punished nonjudicially.[19]

Following the captain's court-martial, General Fogleman "was satisfied that the outcome was appropriate and just; no one was court-martialed who should not have been, or vice-versa, or issued letters of reprimand, Article 15s, and so forth. But I was appalled," he said, "when I asked the question, 'Let me see the evaluation reports on the people.' I discovered that none of what they had done was in those reports."[20] So he personally issued letters of evaluation describing their failure that became a permanent part of each individual's record. For the two F-15 pilots, three officers on the AWACS aircraft, and two generals in the chain of command, this action effectively ended their careers in the Air Force. General

Fogleman also grounded the pilots and AWACS crew members, and disqualified them from duties in flying operations for three years.[21]

Accountability exempts no one. Enlisted members can also be held accountable for failure to perform their unit's mission properly. In May 1995, two Air Force technical sergeants improperly installed and inspected an F-15C fighter's longitudinal and lateral flight control rods. The cross-connected controls caused the plane to roll to the left instead of going up when the stick was pulled back. When the stick was pulled right, instead of rolling right, the plane increased its roll to the left and the nose pitched down. The plane crashed, killing the pilot. Both noncommissioned officers (NCOs) were charged with negligent homicide in the death of the F-15C pilot, as well as four counts each of dereliction of duty for failure to "inspect their work and failure to complete the aircraft maintenance paperwork properly." On the day of his court-martial, the first NCO committed suicide. The second subsequently accepted a general discharge in exchange for dismissal of the charges against him.[22] Accountability, as General Fogleman observed is central to the maintenance of good order and discipline.

Discipline. In his 1944 instructions to the Third Army corps and division commanders, General George S. Patton Jr. declared: "There is only one sort of discipline—perfect discipline. If you do not enforce and maintain discipline, you are potential murderers."[23]

As General Patton's words convey, you face dire consequences if you ignore the issue of discipline. Discipline can be viewed within two frameworks—as an orderly or prescribed conduct or pattern of behavior, or as punishment for failure to meet responsibilities or established standards. Army Regulation 600-20 aptly captures both:

> It [Discipline] is manifested in individuals and units by cohesion, bonding and a spirit of teamwork; by smartness of appearance and action; by cleanliness and maintenance of dress, equipment, and quarters; by deference to seniors and mutual respect between senior and subordinate personnel; by the prompt and willing execution of both the letter and the spirit of the legal orders of their lawful commanders; and by fairness, justice, and equality for all soldiers.[24]

The first framework—an orderly or prescribed conduct of pattern or behavior—begins with self-discipline. Self-discipline is that which, next to virtue, truly and essentially raises one [individual] above another.[25] Self-discipline, which allows you to meet the highest standard without hesitation, is imperative for your success as a commissioned officer. Do what you are told and be where you are supposed to be, when you are supposed to be there, with what you need to accomplish the mission, ready to perform. That is what well and faithfully discharging the duties of the office is all about.

As a military officer, you must act with confidence and cannot indulge yourself in self-pity, discouragement, anger, frustration, or defeatism. You must exercise self-discipline to make decisions and to ensure your loyalties to relationships or personal gain do not supercede loyalty to the Constitution, your service, or the mission.[26]

Self-discipline is displayed via crisp, collective obedience to duly constituted authority, a trait which distinguishes a military organization from a mob. As a military officer, you must respond to orders with alacrity and demand that subordinates follow suit. To achieve compliance effectively, you must retain the separation essential to exercise supreme authority to order men and women into harm's way if need be, with the expectation that you will be obeyed without question. You, in turn, must follow superior direction or rules unless faced with a clear operational, legal, or moral reason to refuse or deviate. At the same time, when necessary, you must be prepared to depart from the letter of instructions to achieve the commander's purpose, justifying these choices to superiors as soon as possible. As always, you are accountable for the consequences of your decisions.

Military discipline is the leader's most important management tool. It is the backbone of efficiency and the essence of an organization.[27] As Patton once remarked, "If you can't get them to salute when they should salute and wear the clothes you tell them to wear, how are you going to get them to die for their country?"[28] You lose your credibility if you fail to hold subordinates consistently accountable for digressing from established standards and policies. Likewise, you must ensure that enforcement of standards is swift, fair, consistent, and impartial if you hope to maintain the effectiveness of your standards and policies.

The second framework of discipline—punishment for failure to meet responsibilities or established standards—is rooted in the UCMJ and the Manual for Courts-Martial.

> The purpose of military law is to promote justice, to assist in maintaining good order and discipline in the armed forces, to promote efficiency and effectiveness in the military establishment, and thereby to strengthen the national security of the United States.[29]

The U.S. Supreme Court, in *Parker* v. *Levy*, 417 U.S. 733, 743 (1974), "has long recognized that the military is, by necessity, a specialized society separate from civilian society."[30] As such, this specialized society operates within a separate military justice system because rules and procedures that may be perfectly suited to the civilian community simply do not meet the needs of military forces who must deploy, live, work, and fight in close and often harsh and dangerous conditions. Furthermore, an armed force has unique legal requirements. There is no civilian legal counterpart to disobedience, absence without leave (AWOL), cowardice, or disrespect.

> An officer is not only an administrator but a magistrate, and it is this dual role which makes his function so radically different than anything encountered in civilian life . . . [M]ilitary discipline . . . is no different than the discipline of the university, a baseball league or a labor union. It makes specific requirements of the individual [and] it has a system of punishments . . . [B]ut the essential difference between discipline in the military establishment and in any other free institution is this, that if the man objects, he still does not have the privilege of quitting tomorrow.[31]

To be effective, the military justice system must be mobile, react to unique offenses, and be administered by those who understand the environment in which it functions.[32] Dr. Douglas McGregor's four-principled "Hot Stove Rule" analogy illustrates how a leader's enforcement of standards and policies provides effective discipline and strengthens leadership's credibility. First, the stove is swift in its message and relatively intense—gives off heat as a warning and "rewards" the offenders immediately. Second, the stove singles out precisely the errant behavior—offenders are not penalized for anything other than the specific deviations. Third, the stove burns all the time; it is consistent—whether you touch it once, twice, or many times the results are the same. Fourth, and final, the stove is impersonal and does not lose its temper—the stove burns indiscriminately anyone who touches it without getting angry or taking it personally.[33]

As a military officer, you have a variety of disciplinary tools available to you, including oral and written counselings, admonitions and reprimands, administrative discharges, nonjudicial punishment, or trial by court-martial. Your base/post legal office will advise you on the particular options pursuant to the respective case, recommend a course of action, and assist you with the appropriate paperwork. Regardless of the offense or desired punishment, you must remain objective, consider each case on its individual merits, and personalize the subsequent action so as to best correct the problem and prevent its recurrence, if possible. The more serious the offense, the heavier the penalty—thus the greater the importance of avoiding injustice by getting all the facts straight, and tempering blind justice with judgment.[34]

The final case study in this chapter captures all of the concepts previously presented, from responsibility, accountability, and lack of self-discipline to full implementation of the military justice system. However, this particular case adds a unique element not discussed in any of the other cases—the impact of our individual actions on relationships with our international allies.

On 3 February 1998, a crew of four Marine captains was aboard a Marine EA-6B, a four-seat electronic warfare aircraft, flying a low-level training mission in the Dolomite Mountains of Calvalese, Italy. On the last leg of the route, the pilot spotted a cable in front of him and saw a yellow flash to his right. The pilot went full-stick forward, negative G, and heard and felt a loud thud. Two cables supporting a ski gondola had sliced into the right wing, creating two large holes and taking off a portion of the vertical stabilizer. When the cables snapped, the gondola fell 370 feet to the ground, killing nine women, 10 men, and one child from Germany, Hungary, Poland, and Italy. On 12 March 1998, a Command Investigation Board, headed by a Marine Corps major general, concluded that aircrew error was the cause of the mishap. The four aircrew members were charged with 20 counts of negligent homicide and several lesser offenses. The commanding officer, executive officer, operations officer, and director of Safety and Standardization faced nonjudicial punishment for systemic errors in the squadron, and the commanding officer was ultimately relieved of command.

Approximately one week after the commanding officer was relieved, investigators discovered that a videotape of portions of the flight existed and had been destroyed by the front right-seater. This revelation came to light when one of the back-seaters was granted immunity and was ordered to testify. Consequently, additional charges of conduct unbecoming an officer were brought against the two front-seaters and were to be handled apart from the courts-martial hearing the negligent homicide charges.

In February 1999, the pilot's General Court-Martial for negligent homicide commenced; he was found not guilty. Subsequently, the charges of negligent homicide were dropped against the right-seater. These results created immense outrage among our Italian allies and the victims' families and governments, who perceived our military justice system as inadequate. Significant international discord within the American and Italian alliance ensued.

In March 1999, the right-seater's General Court-Martial for conduct unbecoming an officer charges was convened to hear the case involving the videotape destruction. The right-seater pleaded guilty and was dismissed from the Marine Corps.[35] When questioned about what he thought of his actions, his response was: "It was the wrong thing. It's not right as a person. It's not right as a Marine Corps [o]fficer. It's not right as [his name]. It was wrong."[36] This Marine captain did the right thing, belatedly, in accepting responsibility for his actions; however, those actions had consequences beyond his own career. They reflected poorly on his service and his country in a large international arena. The "conduct unbecoming an officer" trial for the pilot followed shortly thereafter. He pleaded not guilty. He was convicted and sentenced to six months' confinement and dismissal from the Marine Corps.[37]

The operations in Afghanistan and Iraq that followed the attack on 9/11 have not been without examples of individual officers failing in their responsibilities for expected moral-ethical leadership. An internal investigation traced the scandalous misconduct of a small group of enlisted military police at the Abu Ghraib prison to egregious failures in leadership by the commissioned chain of command of the Army's 800th Military Police Brigade. A number of other unrelated cases have resulted in administrative admonishment, relief, nonjudicial punishment and courts-martial of officers responsible for mistreatment of enemy prisoners, or covering up mistreatment by subordinates, during the stability operations following the successful decapitation of the prewar governments.

Because of these extreme violations of the law and basic disrespect for the humanity of those in our custody, the damage suffered by the nation's international standing is incalculable. "Sad to think," retired Army Colonel James Lacey was quoted as saying, in regard to Abu Ghraib, "that all of this could have been avoided by one strong captain who had a basic education in the difference between right and wrong."[38] What can be said with assurance is that the domestic and international reputations of the armed forces will greatly depend on public opinion—opinion regarding the adequacy of accountability imposed on those commissioned leaders who fail to "well and faithfully discharge" the duties of their office. For those tough ethical decisions, the institutional leadership will ultimately be held accountable.

What all of the aforementioned examples have in common is significant cost to the nation in terms of prestige, national reputation, money, material, and lives suffered as a result of individual inattention, dereliction, or incompetence by relatively junior officers failing, through lack of discipline, to meet their individual and professional responsibilities for precise effective service. Where professionals fail to deliver effective and ethical service, they must expect to face accountability. Where the institution lacks the will to impose it, the profession, and interests of the nation as a whole, suffers. That is the core of General Fogleman's briefing to the Air Force leaders following the judicial processes in the Black Hawk shootdown. You must embrace responsibility, accountability, and discipline, which are defining elements of the officer's profession and vital concepts in keeping with the moral obligations of the oath and the "special trust and confidence" of the nation.

You must not fail.

1. General Sir John Winthrop Hackett, *The Profession of Arms* (New York: Macmillan, 1983), 202.

2. U.S. Department of Defense, *The Armed Forces Officer* (Washington, DC: Government Printing Office, 1950), 2.

3. *Merriam-Webster's Collegiate Dictionary*, Tenth Edition (Springfield, MA: Merriam-Webster, Incorporated, 2001), 8.

4. Tom O'Connor, *Leadership and Accountability*, 1, on-line, Internet, 18 June 2004, available from http://www.amdo.org/leuschnr.html.

5. Colonel Robert Debs Heinl Jr., USMC (Ret.), *Dictionary of Military and Naval Quotations* (Annapolis, MD: United States Naval Institute, 1988), 93. [Heinl errs in dating Washington's letter 1759. Actual date is 29 July 1757.]

6. Captain J. P. Porier, USAF, "Military Justice: History of Military Justice," *Legally Speaking* (Holloman Air Force Base, NM, February 2000), 1.

7. Formal Board of Investigation: Grounding and Loss of USCGC MESQUITE WLB-305, (no date), 44.

8. Ibid., 54.

9. "Collision Summary," 1-2, on-line, Internet, 1 November 2004, available from http://www.cpf.navy.mil/pages/legal/foia/Executive_Summary3.pdf.

10. "Court of Inquiry," 8, on-line, Internet, 1 November 2004, available from http://www.cpf.navy.mil/pages/legal/foia/GREENEVILLE_Combined_COI_Rpt.pdf.

11. "Statement of ADM Tom Fargo, U.S. Pacific Fleet Commander," 2, on-line, Internet, 1 November 2004, available from http://www.cpf.navy.mil/pages/legal/foia/GREENEVILLE_Press_Statements_ADM_Fargo_23_Apr.pdf.

12. "Memorandum for the Record," 3-4, on-line, Internet, 1 November 2004, available from http://www.cpf.navy.mil/pages/legal/foia/COI_Memo_For_the_Record.pdf.

13. "Statement of ADM Fargo," 2-3.

14. Heinl, *Dictionary of Military and Naval Quotations*, 277.

15. "Officer Guilty in Death of Abandoned Marine," (February 26, 1989), 1-2, on-line, Internet, available from http://web.lexis-nexis.com/universe/document?_m=c3dc33b967c4087c43274e2db3655dbb.

16. Lieutenant Colonel Gary E. Slyman, USMC, "Responsibility and Accountability," (U.S. Naval Academy, April 14, 2004), 1-2.

17. Concepts for Air Force Leadership (Maxwell Air Force Base, AL: Air University Press, 2001), 61.

18. General Ronald R. Fogleman, USAF, "Air Force Standards and Accountability," 1, 6, on-line, Internet, 24 April 2004, available from http://www.usafa.af.mil/corevalue/accountability.html.

19. Dr. Richard H. Kohn, "The Early Retirement of Gen Ronald R. Fogleman, Chief of Staff, United States Air Force," *Aerospace Power Journal* (Spring 2001), 14, on-line, Internet, 24 May 2004, available from http://weblinks3.epnet.com/citation.asp?tb=&_ug=sid+4DFDB61C%2D7EAE%2D46B6%2DB96F%2D46CBC37B3DBF%40sessionmgr2+D214&_us=sm+ES+E6C7&_uso=db%5B0+%2Daph+hd+0+op%5B0+%2D+st%5B0+%2DAN++4287548+tg%5B0+%2D+EEE7&.

20. Ibid., 4.

21. Ibid., 14.

22. Lieutenant Colonel J. R. Tillery, USAF, *Accountability: Inconsistent, Situation Dependent and Subjective* (Maxwell Air Force Base, AL: Air University, 1997), 23-26.

23. Heinl, *Dictionary of Military and Naval Quotations*, 94.

24. U.S. Army, Army Regulation 600-20: Army Command Policy (Department of the Army, 13 June 2002), 15.
25. Heinl, *Dictionary of Military and Naval Quotations*, 91.
26. U.S. Air Force Academy, *Officer Development System* (U.S. Air Force Academy, CO, January 2004), 7.
27. Major T. A. Fleek, Lieutenant B. W. Endicott, and Master Sergeant A. R. Orlandella, *Discipline in the Air Force* (Maxwell Air Force Base, AL: Air University Library, June 1955), 8.
28. Heinl, *Dictionary of Military and Naval Quotations*, 94.
29. Manual for Courts-Martial United States, (Washington, DC: Joint Service Committee on Military Justice, 2000), I-1.
30. Mark J. Osiel, *Obeying Orders: Atrocity, Military Discipline and the Law of War* (New Brunswick, NJ: Transaction Publishers, 1999), 164
31. *The Armed Forces Officer* (1950), 139, 143.
32. Porier, "Military Justice,"1-2.
33. Major K. A. Caver, USAF, Major C. A. Franklin, USAF, Major P. H. Henson, USAF, Major S. E. Hirst, USAF, Lieutenant Commander J. C. Jenista, USN, Major S. M. Junkins, Jr., USAF, Lieutenant Commander M. D. McClure, USN, and Major I. S. Phatshwane, USAF, "Ten Propositions Regarding Leadership," Maxwell Air Force Base, AL, on-line, Internet, 4 March 2000, available from http://www.au.af.mil/au/database/projects/ay1996/acsc/96-079.pdf.
34. Major General A. Newman, USA, *Follow Me: The Human Element in Leadership* (Novato, CA: Presidio Press, 1981), 209.
35. Lieutenant Colonel Gary E. Slyman, USMC, "Aviano EA-6B Gondola Mishap (Part A)" (Annapolis, MD: Center for the Study of Professional Military Ethics, U.S. Naval Academy, 25 April 2002), 2.
36. Lieutenant Colonel Gary E. Slyman, USMC, "Aviano EA-6B Gondola Mishap (Part B)" (Annapolis, MD: Center for the Study of Professional Military Ethics, U.S. Naval Academy, 25 April 2002), 3.
37. Slyman, "Part A," 2.
38. Josh White and Thomas E. Ricks, "Top Brass Won't Be Charged Over Abuse: Army Finds Officers Responsible, but Not Culpable, in the Abu Ghraib Scandal," *Washington Post* (27 August 2004), A 17.

CHAPTER 8

SERVICE IDENTITY AND JOINT WARFIGHTING

The Armed Forces of the United States consist of five military services—the Air Force, the Army, the Coast Guard, the Marine Corps, and the Navy. In the twenty-first century, the days of any service operating as a truly independent actor are long since past. The five services fight together as a team, which means they must plan and train as a team. That does not mean that all five play equal parts in every battle or exercise. It does mean that the five are partners in the overall business of defending the United States, its territory, population, and national interests, and, therefore, that the best each has to offer must be woven into every battle, exercise, and plan. There can be no "lone wolves" among our five services, because our security cannot afford such free agentry. When the nation is threatened, the Navy doesn't go to war, nor does the Army; the nation goes to war, using all its services' capabilities in the combination that best suits the particular threat posed and the war plan designed to defeat it.

While "jointness" has become the short-hand description for this five-service partnership, with its own color—purple—there is another way to characterize the relationship among the services, one with deep roots in American history and political culture—*E pluribus unum*—From many, one. Inscribed on the banner held in the beak of the eagle on the Great Seal of the United States, approved by Congress on 20 June 1782, those words convey the reality that out of the original 13 colonies, one nation emerged. The 13 new states kept their own identities, as well as their own local customs, food preferences, accents, and so forth, but together they constituted one nation that was not just the sum of the 13, but greater than the total when combined.

So, too, from five services comes the one entity—the Armed Forces of the United States—charged with the defense of the nation.

Tradition and identity, including uniforms and customs, matter, as do the requirements generated by the distinctive roles the various services perform; the requirements involved in fighting on land, at sea, and in the air; and the different capabilities they bring to the battle. Thus, the services keep their separate traditions and identities, their distinctive uniforms and customs, but out of the five of them emerges a single armed force that, because of the synergies among them, is greater, more flexible, and more capable than the mere sum of the five.

This book is all about being an officer in the Armed Forces of the United States in the early years of the twenty-first century. That involves being an officer in the Air Force, Army, Coast Guard, Marine Corps, or Navy, while also being an officer in something larger—the Armed Forces of the United States. To be a fully effective officer, both in one service and in the armed forces, requires knowing one's own service well, including its capabilities as well as its limitations, and knowing the other services well enough to appreciate their strengths and their weaknesses, what they bring to the fight, and how their capabilities can best mesh with those of the other services.

Each service has its own uniforms, customs, and traditions. On a deeper level, each has its own culture. It is culture that defines and describes any organization best. It also best defines and describes what it means to be a member of that organization. Thus, part of this chapter's contribution to understanding what it means to be an officer in the armed forces is to capture, albeit in snapshot style, the culture of each of the five services. As used here, culture is taken to have two meanings—on the organizational level, how this service defines and sees itself; and on the individual level, what it means to be an Airman, a Soldier, a Coast Guardsman, a Marine, or a Sailor.

The Air Force. "Man's flight through life is sustained by the power of his knowledge." These words, written by Austin "Dusty" Miller and found on the Eagle and Fledglings statue at the U.S. Air Force Academy, introduce Air Force service culture. At the heart of this culture is the idea that aviation transformed both civil society and warfare. Aircraft revolutionized war by adding a third dimension to land and sea operations, along with unmatched speed, range, mobility, and flexibility in both combat and support activities. In a like manner, evolving space technology transforms warfare on the earth's surface. Space capabilities provide revolutionary strides in global presence; intelligence, surveillance, and reconnaissance (ISR); communications; geo-location; navigation; weather; and precision weaponry. The airplane and spacecraft also dramatically changed society by opening new horizons of knowledge and shattering previous barriers of time and distance. They made the world smaller. The realities of technology's impact fundamentally altered how we travel, how we view the world, and how we fight.

Current Air Force culture emphasizes the term "Airman." In the past, this word referred to pilots and navigators, but now Airman refers to anyone who understands and appreciates the full range of air and space capabilities and can employ or support some aspect of airpower and space power. The Air Force understands that not all Airmen wear a blue uniform; some wear green or khaki. Some fight from ships. Moreover, in today's world, nonflying space operators, maintainers, intelligence personnel, supply troops, and other support functions prove vital to air and space superiority. They are Airmen and form the air and space team.

The concept of independence formed the bedrock of Air Force identity in its early days. Pioneer Airmen believed that the air arm must achieve service independence in order to operate most effectively and provide the single-minded focus to maximize airpower's potential. At the core of that belief was their understanding, gained through theory and experience, of the strengths and weaknesses of airpower and space power. Early airpower theory stressed strategic airpower, the ability to destroy an enemy's war-making capability by attacking vital centers of industrial or communications infrastructure.

Although strategic attack remains an important operational function of air and space power, contemporary air and space doctrine emphasizes support to joint and multinational operations. It describes the contribution of air and space power to the joint warfighting team through "the tenets of air and space power." According to AFDD 1, Air Force Basic Doctrine, airpower and space power:

- Should be centrally controlled and decentrally executed
- Is flexible and versatile
- Produces synergistic effects
- Offers a unique form of persistence
- Must be prioritized
- Must be balanced

These tenets reflect the specific lessons of air and space operations over history and require informed judgment in application.[1]

On the other hand, historically there were inherent limitations of airpower, and these too were recognized early in the airplane's development:

- Technology and capital dependent—not every country has the industrial, scientific or financial resources to build modern aircraft
- Transitory—aircraft cannot live in their medium as can surface forces; aircraft must land to refuel and rearm. ...
- Weather and night—the natural phenomena of rain, wind, clouds, and darkness of night present formidable barriers to flight
- Cannot hold ground—for surface advocates this is the most damning limitation; only troops can occupy and, therefore, control events on the ground[2]

Over the past century of flight, technology enhanced airpower's strengths and diminished its traditional weaknesses. While space assets do not share the same limitations, scientific, technological, and budgetary obstacles pose challenges. Today's Air Force emphasizes mastery of the capabilities and potential of airpower and space power, while understanding fully their limitations. Along the same lines, in order to appreciate Air Force service culture, an officer should comprehend the following ideas that mark the Air Force vision:

- **Unity of command and centralized control/decentralized execution.** Airmen still believe that the Air Force is the service most oriented to think in strategic, operational, and tactical dimensions; to think globally; to appreciate and emphasize time; hence, Airmen should work for Airmen and the senior Airman should work for the geographic combatant commander (theater commander) to maximize the capabilities of the joint service team.

- **Future-oriented and technology-focused.** Advances in technology dominate both the official and unofficial service culture of the Air Force. In one sense, Air Force personnel tend to identify with their plane, space system, or service specialty. Since it often takes years to master the technology and procedures involved, this cultural trait is natural, but today's Air Force emphasizes a common mission and doctrine to minimize division. Additionally, since rapid technological advances dominate air war, Airmen believe in the words of one of the pioneers of airpower theory, Italian Air Marshal Giulio Douhet: "Victory smiles upon those who anticipate the changes in the character of war, not upon those who wait to adapt themselves after the changes occur."[3]

- **Space—unlimited horizons.** With scientific advances opening exciting vistas of space, Douhet's remark captures Air Force thinking for the twenty-first century. Today's Airman appreciates the value of space as "the ultimate high-ground" and views American space supremacy as an imperative. Today's Air Force is committed to developing tomorrow's space capability in three vital areas: an unsurpassed military and civilian space cadre; a strong and consistently funded space industrial base; and a commitment to leading-edge space research and exploration.[4] Thus, today's Air Force considers itself a genuine air and space force.

- **Adaptability and change.** From the dawn of flight, Airmen understood the vital role of nonmilitary aviation. The founders of the U.S. Air Force consciously developed ties to civilian aerospace industry and the airlines, as well as to popular culture, in an attempt to develop "air mindedness" and public acceptance. Like civilian industry, the Air Force is based on adaptability and change; new ideas are encouraged; new management trends are often adopted.

- **Expeditionary and forward deployed.** For most of its first 50 years, the Air Force conducted global operations from fixed bases within the Continental United States (CONUS) or overseas. With the end of the Cold War and a rise in overseas contingency operations, Air Force culture and operations shifted to an expeditionary, forward-deployed reality. Concentrating on rapid, effective deployment, barebase operations, and crisis-response actions, the Air and Space Expeditionary Force represents not only a new organization and training focus, but a new attitude.[5]

With a shorter service history, fewer cherished traditions, more emphasis on change, the Air Force often struggles with service identity. At times, officers and enlisted personnel master their individual service specialties and become highly skilled, but overly specialized, and lose perspective on broader service concerns. Nevertheless, the Air Force prides itself on mission focus and accomplishment. Air Force culture looks to the future and attempts to lead technological trends.

The Army. The Army exists to serve the Nation.[6] Throughout its history, the U.S. Army mission has remained constant: to secure and defend our homeland and decisively defeat those enemies who strive to disrupt our freedoms. The birth of the U.S. Army preceded the birth of the Nation. One of the first actions undertaken by the Continental Congress on 14 June 1775—before that gathering began even considering a Declaration of Independence—was to direct General George Washington to muster troops for a Continental Army. That army, along with colonial militias, defeated the British in the eight-year War of Independence.[7] Today, as part of the joint force, the Army continues to support and defend America's Constitution and way of life. The Army protects national security interests, including forces, possessions, citizens, allies and friends. It prepares for and delivers decisive action in all operations. Above all, the Army provides combatant commanders with versatile land forces ready to fight and win the Nation's wars.[8]

The Army's contribution to joint operations is landpower. Landpower is the ability—by threat, force, or occupation—to promptly gain, sustain, and exploit control over land, resources, and people. Landpower includes the ability to:

- Impose the Nation's will on adversaries—by force if necessary—in diverse and complex terrain
- Establish and maintain a stable environment that sets the conditions for a lasting peace
- Address the consequences of catastrophic events—both natural and man-made—to restore infrastructure and reestablish basic civil services

- Support and provide a base from which forces can influence and dominate the air and sea dimensions of the joint operational area[9]

Ultimately, Army forces' ability to control land, resources, and people through a sustained presence makes permanent the advantages gained by joint forces.[10] Army forces provide combatant commanders the means to deter potential adversaries and shape the strategic environment.[11]

Several factors underlie the credibility and capability that make Army Forces relevant in any environment. Tough disciplined Soldiers and imaginative, adaptive leadership are essential. Rigorous and realistic training, sound doctrine, and modern equipment also contribute. The design and practices of Army institutional structures provide essential support. These same characteristics make Army forces important to establishing relationships with potential multinational partners. The versatile mix of Army organizations provides combatant commanders with the landpower necessary to achieve objectives across the range of military operations.[12]

While the core Army mission has changed little over the years, the Army has adapted to the evolving nature and pace of conflict. Current Army transformation efforts focus on requirements for fighting and winning the global war on terrorism and meeting other national security and defense missions, while simultaneously posturing the Army to sustain its full range of global commitments into the future.[13] The future Army will embody several key attributes as it becomes a force that is more joint and expeditionary, adaptive and flexible, lethal and survivable.

Campaign Quality Army. Recent conflicts have demonstrated that the duration and nature of Army "boots on the ground" is inherently unpredictable. The campaign quality of an Army thus is not only its ability to win decisive combat operations, but also its ability to sustain those operations as long as necessary, adapting them as required to unpredictable and often profound changes in the context and character of the conflict. The Army's preeminent challenge is to reconcile expeditionary agility and responsiveness with the staying power, durability, and adaptability to carry a conflict to a victorious conclusion no matter what form it eventually takes.[14]

Expeditionary Mindset. In this globalized world, our enemies shift resources and activities to areas least accessible to our armed forces. As elusive and adaptive enemies seek refuge in the far corners of the earth, the norm will be short-notice operations, at great distance, in extremely austere theaters of operations, with incomplete information available. These conditions define expeditionary operations. Soldiers with an expeditionary mindset will be confident that they are organized, trained, and equipped to go anywhere in the world, at any time, in any environment, against any adversary, and accomplish the assigned mission.[15]

A Joint Mindset. Our collective future is irrefutably joint. To meet the challenges of expeditionary operations, the Army can and must embrace the capabilities of its sister services right down to the tactical level. That will require development of operational concepts, capabilities and training programs that are joint from the outset.[16] This in turn requires a new emphasis on individual leadership and values.

First and foremost, the Army is Soldiers.[17] Soldiers have always, and will remain, the Army's centerpiece—the basic building block of all Army organizations and operations. The Army's greatness as an institution and its reputation around the world is derived from the values and actions of its Soldiers. Living the Warrior Ethos and inspired by the Army's enduring traditions and heritage, Soldiers are the best citizens the nation has to offer.

Warrior Ethos.[18] As in the past, Soldiers serving the Nation today embody the Warrior Ethos:

- I will always place the mission first
- I will never accept defeat
- I will never quit
- I will never leave a fallen comrade

The Army seeks individuals ready and willing for warrior service. Bound to each other by integrity and trust, the young Americans welcomed into the Army learn that in the Army every Soldier is a leader, responsible for what happens in his or her presence regardless of rank. They value learning and adaptability, particularly as it contributes to initiative. They learn the Army's culture is one of values, and that Soldiers adhere to the following seven core Army values: loyalty, duty, respect, selfless service, honor, integrity and personal courage.

Soldier's Creed.[19] In addition to the seven core values, all Soldiers are expected to uphold a set of principles called the Soldier's Creed. This guides every aspect of their Army lives, from their behavior and attitude to their training and the carrying out of duties and missions. The Warrior Ethos and the Soldier's Creed form the moral and ethical content of America's Army.[20]

I am an American Soldier.
I am a Warrior and a member of a team. I serve the people of
he United States and live the Army Values. I will always place the mission first.
I will never accept defeat. I will never quit. I will never leave a fallen comrade.
I am disciplined, physically and mentally tough, trained and proficient in my
warrior tasks and drills. I always maintain my arms, my equipment and myself.
I am an expert and I am a professional. I stand ready to deploy, engage and

destroy the enemies of the United States of America in close combat.
I am a guardian of freedom and the American way of life.
I am an American Soldier.

The Coast Guard.

In 1790, the First Congress of the United States established a small maritime law enforcement agency to assist in collecting the new nation's customs duties. For the next eight years this Revenue Marine (later called the Revenue Cutter Service) was the nation's only naval force and so was soon assigned military duties. Over time, the Revenue Cutter Service acquired new responsibilities ... the result is today's U. S. Coast Guard–a unique force that carries out an array of civil and military responsibilities touching on almost every facet of the maritime environment. ...

... the Coast Guard's legal historical core is as a military service, originated with unique law enforcement authority and leavened with a well-earned reputation for humanitarian service. These purposeful attributes enable us to meet a broad multimission mandate from our nation. Our core values of honor, respect, and devotion to duty enable that mandate to be fulfilled. As America's Maritime Guardian, we are proud to be warriors and protectors at all times.

—Coast Guard Publication 1

The Coast Guard's Foundation Doctrine articulates the essence of the nation's smallest branch of the armed forces. Two hundred plus years as the only armed service assigned a vast array of civil responsibilities and missions has caused the Coast Guard's culture to be distinctly different from its four larger military cousins. The nation has long recognized that the Coast Guard requires military discipline and training to perform its national defense duties and its often dangerous maritime security and safety missions successfully. When Alexander Hamilton originally suggested forming the Revenue Marine, he insisted on organizing it along military lines and convinced President Washington to commission Revenue Marine officers. Thus began the formation of the military culture and history of this small, distinct naval service.

To understand the Coast Guard's unique service culture, one must recognize that it is the compilation of several interrelated histories and cultures. Formed in 1915 when its parent organization, the U.S. Revenue Cutter Service, combined with the U.S. Life Saving Service, the Coast Guard would later absorb the U.S. Lighthouse Service and the Bureau of Maritime Inspection and Navigation. The distinctive service that exists today includes attributes and core values from each organization, expanding and strengthening the Coast Guard's maritime culture.

Here are a few highlights of the things that form Coast Guard culture today:

- *A naval service:* The Coast Guard is a naval service. It honors the same naval ceremonies, customs, and traditions as its larger sea service cousins. From the titles it attaches to its ranks and rates, to the nautical nomenclature used in everyday speech, the Coast Guard shares a common maritime history with sailors everywhere. Coast Guardsmen have a deep affection for the sea and its lore. Coast Guard cutters are U.S. warships. The cuttermen who sail in these ships continue a long and distinguished seagoing heritage. Having fought side by side at home and abroad in every conflict in U.S. history, the Coast Guard is inspired by the history and tradition of the U.S. Navy as well as its own.

- *All things maritime:* The Coast Guard's many roles and missions require it to possess a rare blend of humanitarian, law enforcement, regulatory, diplomatic, and military capabilities. The Coast Guard's many broad regulatory mandates require it to monitor and understand all manner of activity on or near the water. This omnipresence provides a "cop on the beat" like familiarity with the waterfront and a deep understanding of the many occupations and enterprises that make their living on or around the sea. A long, distinguished history of enforcing international maritime treaties and successful joint naval operations extends this comprehensive knowledge and understanding of all things maritime far beyond the borders of the U.S. The Coast Guard and its unique military, multimission, maritime culture provide a model for naval services around the world.

- *Face to face interaction with the citizens it serves:* The Coast Guard's many civil, peacetime missions require it to have far greater day-to-day interaction with the American public than the other branches of the armed forces. From rescuing a recreational boater in distress, to conducting an inspection on a large merchant ship, many citizens have reason to have routine contact with Coast Guard personnel. This frequent interaction presents extraordinary challenges for the organization and the individual Coast Guardsman. Coast Guard personnel must exercise their powers prudently and with restraint. In his 1791 Letter of Instruction to Revenue Cutter officers, Alexander Hamilton charged them to "overcome difficulties by cool and temperate perseverance to [your] duty." That standard remains integral to Coast Guard culture today.

- *Small units in small places:* The Coast Guard has very few large bases. It is an organization dominated by small boat stations, small cutters (ships), and small air stations—often in similarly small coastal communities far from other military facilities. These small units are integral parts of the community. Often operating far from higher command authority, junior Coast Guard leaders enjoy a clear mandate for on-scene initiative, but also bear immense responsibility for the well being and conduct of their crews.

- ***"You have to go out but you don't have to come back":*** Coast Guardsmen are taught to avoid or mitigate unnecessary risk, but this historic, deep-rooted saying from the U.S. Lifesaving Service captures the Coast Guard's heritage of selfless service to the nation. Be it combat, law enforcement, or search and rescue operations, the Coast Guard does dangerous work in hostile environments. Selfless acts by courageous men and women using their tools and their wits under dangerous conditions to get the job done are the foundation of Coast Guard culture. A lifeboat crashing through the surf or a helicopter in a low hover over a vessel in distress are the enduring images of the Coast Guard at work.

- ***Maritime Cop on the Beat:*** Maritime law enforcement and border control are the oldest of the Coast Guard's many responsibilities and is the historic core of its existence. Stopping and boarding ships at sea provided the foundation upon which the Coast Guard's broader and more complex present-day mission set is built. The burden of being the nation's primary maritime law enforcement service is an essential and inescapable component of Coast Guard culture.

- ***Lifesaver, Guardian and Warrior:*** The sacred triad of the Coast Guardsman's persona and psyche is that of lifesaver, guardian, and warrior.[21] Every Coast Guardsman must be all three at all times—they are not privileged to pick and choose. A law enforcement patrol can become a search and rescue sortie or emergent response to a security threat at a moments notice. The call to deploy the Coast Guard's unique skills to a foreign shore may come at any time. Every Coast Guardsman must remain Semper Paratus—always ready—to answer the call.

The Coast Guard's relatively small size, assignment as a Tier One organization in the Department of Homeland Security, and civil responsibilities and missions make its culture unparalleled among the U.S. Armed Forces.

What makes the Coast Guard unique is that in executing our diverse missions as America's Maritime Guardian, we harmonize what seem to be contradictory mandates. We are charged at once to be policemen and sailors, warriors, humanitarians, regulators, stewards of the environment, diplomats, and guardians of the coast. Thus we are military, multimission, and maritime.

—Coast Guard Publication 1

Marine Corps. There are no ex-Marines: "Once a Marine, Always a Marine." Marines are different. They have their own air arm and deploy on land and at sea. They have the longest boot camp. They have a hymn, not a song. Marines are different because of their ethos.

Chapter 1 of Fleet Marine Force Manual-1-0 is titled "Our Ethos." On the first page it states:

> ... being a Marine comes from the eagle, globe, and anchor that is tattooed on the soul of every one of us who wears the Marine Corps uniform. ... Unlike physical or psychological scars, which over time, tend to heal and fade in intensity, the eagle, globe, and anchor only grow more defined–more intense–the longer you are a Marine. 'Once a Marine, always a Marine.'[22]

That tattoo is a selfless spirit of being one of the few. Ask any member of the Marine Corps what he or she does, and the answer will be, "I'm a Marine." What is most important to a Marine is being a Marine, not what rank or military occupational specialty he or she holds. It is the culture of the Marine Corps that makes the Corps different from society as a whole, as well as from the other services. Its deep appreciation for its rich history and traditions instills pride and responsibility in every Marine down to the lowest levels. Every Marine has celebrated the Marine Corps Birthday every year since becoming a Marine, whether in garrison or in combat. In garrison, it is celebrated every year everywhere in the world with the identical ceremony. Older Marines pass the traditions of the Corps to younger ones, ensuring they understand that the successes and sacrifices of the past set the path for the future. Since the first two battalions of Marines were raised by an act of the Continental Congress in 1775, many of whom were recruited from Tun Tavern in Philadelphia, Pennsylvania, the Corps has distinguished itself in every conflict in our nation's history.

"Every Marine is a Rifleman": In fact, every Marine officer or enlisted is trained first to be a rifleman before being trained in any other specialty. It is this bedrock premise of "every Marine a rifleman" and the training that goes with it that set all Marines on a common foundation. Leaders are molded in the same training given those they will lead, building empathy and understanding unattainable in other services. Every facet of the Marine Corps exists to support the Marine rifleman, and every Marine understands that.

"Soldiers of the Sea": It is the culture of the Marine Corps that produces the Soldier of the Sea. The Marine Corps is determined to be different—in military appearance, obedience to orders, disciplined behavior, adherence to traditions, and most important, the unyielding conviction that the Corps exists to fight.[23]

"Taking Care of Our Own": The characteristic that best defines Marines is selflessness: a spirit that places the self-interest of the individual after that of the institution and the team, all working toward a common goal. It is important that the unit succeed, not the individual. It is common to hear Marines speak of their leaders based on how well they take care of subordinates. "Take care of your people" and "Take care of each other" are imbued in Marines from the

first day. Officers eat last. They inspect the chow hall by eating in it. They know how their troops live in the barracks because they go there, and in the field they never have more creature comforts than their troops do. The only privilege of rank is that of ensuring that your subordinates are cared for. This culture defines what the Marine Corps is and who Marines are—men and women who exhibit extraordinary leadership and courage, both physical and moral, shaped by their dedication to the institution and each other.

"Combined Arms Expeditionary Forces in Readiness": Operationally there are four generally accepted characteristics that define and describe the Marine Corps. First, although capable of deploying and employing by various means, the specialty is amphibious: the Corps comes from the sea. Therefore, it focuses primarily on the coastal or littoral regions of the world. Second, the Marine Corps trains and operates as a Marine air-ground task force, a combined-arms, air-ground team, logistically self-sustainable. Third, as a force-in-readiness, the Marine Corps is a national "swing force"—forward deployed and expeditionary by nature—ready to respond rapidly to crises. Fourth, the Marine Corps considers itself a light-to-medium force, packing a quick and lethal punch. Although prepared to operate across the full conflict spectrum, the Marine Corps is more at home and most effective as a light-to-medium force that can be on-scene quickly with enough firepower and sustainability to conduct operations as an "enabling force" until heavier units arrive.

The Marine Corps is small. In 2004, only 211,000 active and Reserve (171,286 active duty), of which more than 114,000 are in the operating forces and more than 35,000 are typically forward-deployed. As part of its expeditionary nature, the operating forces of the Marine Corps live on "camps," not forts or bases, and maintain a high tooth-to-tail ratio, relying on the other services for a large portion of logistics, transportation, education, and combat service support. Many Marines receive specialized training at the other services' schools. There are no Marine doctors, nurses, dentists, field medical corpsmen, or chaplains (all of whom are provided by the Navy). The Air Force and the Navy get the Marines to the fight, with the Army assisting toward sustainment if Marines are forward-deployed beyond 90 days.

Seventy percent of active duty Marine forces are in the operating forces, with the bulk of those forces in the Fleet Marine Forces. These operating forces provide the combat power that is immediately available to the combatant commanders for employment.

To Marines "expeditionary" means more than just getting there quickly. The Marines in the operating forces, most in a Spartan-like "temporary-residence" mindset when not deployed, are eager members of the combined-arms team. This team is tailored toward a maneuver warfare approach to combat, where power from the sea is projected across the littoral, ideally maximizing the combined effect of its resources at a critical seam of the enemy's defense.

In 1957 the Commandant of the Marine Corps asked Lieutenant General Victor Krulak, "Why does the United States need a Marine Corps?" Five days later General Krulak replied:

Essentially, as a result of the unfailing conduct of our Corps over the years, they (our nation's citizens) believe three things about Marines. First they believe when trouble comes to our country there will be Marines— somewhere—who, through hard work, have made and kept themselves ready to do some thing useful about it, and do it at once. ...

Second, they believe that when the Marines go to war they invariably turn in a performance that is dramatically and decisively successful—not most of the time, but always. Their faith and their convictions in this regard are almost mystical....

The third thing they believe about Marines is that our Corps is downright good for ... our country; that the Marines are masters of a form of unfailing alchemy which converts unoriented youths into proud, self-reliant stable citizens—citizens into whose hands the nation's affairs may safely be entrusted.[24]

Krulak went on to conclude:

I believe the burden of all this can be summarized by saying that, while the functions which we discharge must always be done by someone, and while an organization such as ours is the correct one to do it, still, in terms of cold mechanical logic, the United States does not need a Marine Corps. However, for good reasons which completely transcend logic, the United States wants a Marine Corps. Those reasons are strong; they are honest, they are deep rooted and they are above question or criticism. So long as they exist—so long as the people are convinced that we can really do the three things I mentioned—we are going to have a Marine Corps. ... And, likewise, should the people ever lose that conviction—as a result of our failure to meet their high—almost spiritual standards—the Marine Corps will then quickly disappear.[25]

In 1935 Gunnery Sergeant Walter Holzworth was asked how the Marine Corps came by its reputation as one of the world's greatest fighting formations. He replied, "Well, they started right out telling everybody how great they were. Pretty soon they got to believing it themselves. And they have been busy ever since proving they were right."[26]

The Navy. "The profound influence of sea commerce upon the wealth and strength of countries was clearly seen long before the true principles which governed its growth and prosperity were decided," wrote Alfred Thayer Mahan on page 1 of his classic, *The Influence of Sea Power upon History, 1660–1783.*[27] "Mahan's studies convinced him that sea power, conceived on a broader scale, would constitute for the United States ... an instrument of policy serving to enhance the nation's power and prestige."[28]

Like many other navies, the U.S. Navy has always seen itself as intimately tied to national power—protecting it, enhancing it, advancing it. From the seed of this idea has grown the rich heritage that has shaped the way the Navy has done business for centuries, on any of "the seven seas." As a seagoing service, the Navy is built on combat ships and aircraft, supported by a seaborne logistics force, protecting U.S. interests at sea and on the land immediately adjacent to the sea. And the culture of the Navy is built on this idea, shaped by—and shaping—this rich heritage.

Those who go down to the sea in ships: The Navy and its Sailors go to sea. For Sailors, tours at sea and tours ashore are two different things entirely. The first are "what it's all about"; the latter are the interludes between cruises. Sailors often pride themselves, indeed brag about, how many months or years of their career they have spent at sea. The oceans are vast, and ships move slowly, so tours at sea are long, usually measured in months rather than weeks. The Navy culture is a deployment culture; deployments form the rhythm of Navy life for the Sailors and for their families. If "home is where the heart is," then many, perhaps most, Sailors have two homes—the one with family and friends ashore and the other with shipmates on deployment.

The Navy's worldwide presence and availability "on the seven seas" are its hallmarks and make it usually the "first on the scene" when trouble erupts affecting U.S. interests in any corner of the globe. To this day, the Navy says, and on some level believes, that when a crisis springs up, the first question the president of the United States asks is, "Where are the carriers?"

Independence: The Navy has always been the most independent of the armed services. During the Navy's formative years, when a ship went to sea, it cut nearly all its ties to its place of origin. The oftentimes harsh nature of the operating environment at sea forces the Navy to a culture of self-reliance. In the days before modern communications, when the captain of a ship at sea surveyed the horizons from the bridge, he was literally the master of all he surveyed. There was no one else, including superior officers, there.

Autonomy of command at sea: The captain, thus, was the sole word of authority aboard the ship, and every decision rested squarely on his shoulders. Even after electronics created the ability to "talk to the boss" around the clock, anywhere in the world, the habit of autonomous operations continued to reside in the naval forces. "Command by Negation," a concept unique to naval command and control, allows a subordinate commander the freedom to operate as he or she sees best, keeping authorities informed of decisions taken, until the senior overrides a decision. The Navy is the only service that uses the acronym UNODIR (UNless Otherwise DIRected) by which a commanding officer informs the boss of a proposed course of action, and only if the boss overrides it, will it not be taken. The subordinate is informing the boss, not asking permission.

Community subcultures: One other important element of the Navy culture does not have ancient roots, but is rather a function of the evolution of the Navy and, to a great extent, the evolution of technology and hardware. More so than members of the other services, the Sailor identifies with a specific warfare specialty or community. The Army has its infantry, artillery, and armor officers, for example, but the centripetal force of the surface, submarine, aviation, and special warfare communities in the Navy exceeds anything their comrades in arms in other uniforms know. While some of this power comes from parochialism, there is a more substantial reason for it. No matter their branch, all Army officers operate on, or very near to, the ground. Land warfare is their specialty; they work on the ground. In contrast, some naval officers operate on the surface of the water, some underneath it, others fly high above it, and still others use the water as the springboard for special operations on land: different warfare community, different medium in which they operate. They think differently because they have to—the varying mediums in which they operate demand it.

Surface officers see themselves as the "backbone" of the naval service, involved in all facets of our nation's defense from power projection ashore to maritime interdiction operations and law enforcement. Submariners take pride in being known as the "Silent Service," referring not only to the stealthiness of their platform, but also to their culture of not discussing their specific operations with others. Since 1910 when the first naval officer was ordered to flight training, naval aviators have assumed an increasingly important role in the Navy, and with it, a style in many ways more like those of their fellow aviators in other services than like those of their fellow Sailors in the surface, submarine, or special warfare communities. The SEALs (Sea, Air, Land) embody both a flexibility beyond that of their fellow Sailors and a bond between officers and enlisted that is unique within the Navy; this latter is both the reason for and the product of the single Basic Underwater Demolition/SEAL (BUD/S) course that all SEAL officers and enlisted must complete.

Navy-Marine Corps Team. One further element of the Navy culture has to do with its close linkage to the Marine Corps. With both branches united under the Department of the Navy, sharing one academy as a commissioning source, and bearing a history of partnership dating back to the eighteenth century, the Navy-Marine Corps team is able not only to influence events at sea, but also to project power ashore, defending and advancing U.S. interests around the world.

❖   ❖   ❖

E pluribus unum. These five, powerful services, diverse but complementary, constitute the armed forces. The challenge for the armed forces officer is to be simultaneously a master of his or her own service and a knowledgeable partner of the other four. Taking appropriate pride in one's own service is in order, but that should never stray into arrogance regarding the other services. Different does not mean inferior. It means different. The talented, professional officer—at any pay grade—must be ready, willing, and able to leverage the best of each of the services, as the mission requires.

Joint warfighting is the employment of all the armed forces in a common effort to achieve a desired end. Joint warfighting is not new to the American armed forces. Washington's victory at Yorktown depended on cooperation with naval forces (i.e., the French fleet). Grant's victories on the western rivers were built largely on Navy cooperation with Army forces onshore. The great amphibious landings of World War II could not have taken place without imaginative and detailed integration of the efforts and complementary capabilities of all the nation's military forces.

What has changed in the twenty-first century is the overlapping nature of individual service capabilities within a single area of operations. Essentially, the range of weapons and communication systems, combined with the ability to create and operate sophisticated information networks, promises to reduce the theater of war to a single battlefield on which effects created by forces of all services can be employed selectively and simultaneously throughout the area, much as Napoleon directed subordinate units around early nineteenth-century battlefields.

As Napoleon's cavalry, artillery, and infantry retained unique characters because of differences in capabilities, operating requirements, and skills, so today's military services necessarily retain their unique identities, founded both on their histories and on the continuing differences in the functional require-ments of operating in their respective mediums. Conflicting pressures—full operational integration of effects for greatest collective impact and organiza-tional separation to maximize individual means—have required the development of new organizational concepts to guide the services in achieving the greatest possible operational integration, while maintaining their more or less traditional organizational diversity.

Central to twenty-first century warfare by the U.S. Armed Forces is the concept of joint interdependence, broadly the notion that service capabilities provided to joint operational commanders are combined to achieve their full complementary effects, at the lowest possible level, to obtain the greatest possible collective effects.[29] Achieving joint interdependence requires that junior officers understand the differing strengths and limitations of each service's capabilities and know how to integrate those capabilities in their actions to speed mission accomplishment. Service rivalries have no place on the battlefield, where success, not credit, is the professional currency.

Because seamless cooperation at all levels is increasingly important, reciprocal respect of members of other services as fellow warriors and officers is vital. Operational integration begins with mutual understanding and respect, as well as shared adherence to the ethic born out of the common oath and commission which this book takes as its substantive starting point. Joint synergy, the ability to make the whole greater than the sum of the parts, begins with understanding the several service cultures: *E pluribus unum*.

1. AFDD 1, Air Force Basic Doctrine, 17 November 2003, 27. In a related explanation, contemporary airpower theorist retired Colonel Phillip S. Meilinger expressed airpower's inherent strengths as Ubiquity—the ability to operate in the third dimension above the Earth, unconstrained by the limitations of terrain; Speed—an order of magnitude faster than their surface counterparts; Range—truly global; Potency—while striking deeply in an enemy country, aircraft can deliver significant ordinance; Flexibility—the combination of above factors that allow aircraft to perform a variety of missions, over a wide area, in a very short period of time, Philip S. Meilinger, *Airwar: Theory and Practice* (London: Frank Cass, 2003), 1-2.

2. Meilinger, *Airwar*, 1-2.

3. Giulio Douhet, *The Command of the Air*, trans. Dino Ferrari (New York: Coward-McCann, 1942; reprint, Washington, DC: Office of Air Force History, 1983), 30.

4. Peter B. Teats, "The Road to Space Supremacy," Address to Air Force Association Air and Space Conference 2004, 14 September 2004, Washington, DC, on-line, Internet, 13 October 2004, available from http://www.afa.org/media/scripts/Supremacy_Conf.html.

5. General John P. Jumper, "Chief's Sight Picture: The Culture of our Air and Space Expeditionary Force and the Value of Air Force Doctrine," Air Force email distribution, 5 July 2003; General John P. Jumper, "Chief's Sight Picture: Adapting the AEF—Longer Deployments, More Forces," Air Force email distribution, 4 June 2004.

6. At the request of the Army Staff, the discussion of The Army, which follows, is taken largely verbatim from *FM 1, The Army*, June 2005, and the 2004 Department of the Army Pamphlet, *Serving a Nation at War: A Campaign Quality Army with Joint and Expeditionary Mindset*.

7. Profile of the United States Army, a reference handbook 2005, Association of the Unites States Army, 13

8. FM 1, The Army, 1-1.

9. Ibid.
10. Ibid.
11. Ibid, 3-4.
12. Ibid, 1-1, 1-2.
13. "Building the Future Force While Continuing to Fight The Global War on Terrorism," Dr Francis J. Harvey, Secretary of the Army, article in October 2005 *Army* magazine.
14. "Department of the Army White Paper, Serving a Nation at War: A Campaign Quality Army with Joint and Expeditionary Capabilities," (28 April 2004), 7.
15. Ibid., 4, 5.
16. Ibid., 5-6.
17. *FM 1, The Army*, 1-1.
18. U.S. Army homepage – www.army.mil.
19. Ibid.
20. See Chapter 1, *FM 1, The Army*.
21. Captain Bruce Stubbs, "We Are Lifesavers, Guardian, and Warriors," *Proceedings*, U.S. Naval Institute (April 2002).
22. *Leading Marines*, FMFM1-0 (Washington DC: Department of the Navy, Headquarters, U.S. Marine Corps, 1995), 7.
23. Ibid., 8.
24. Victor H. Krulak, *First to Fight: An Inside View of the United States Marine Corps* (New York: Pocket Books, 1984), xix-xxi.
25. Ibid., xx-xxi.
26. Ibid., 1.
27. Alfred Thayer Mahan, *The Influence of Sea Power upon History, 1660–1783* (New York: Dover Publications, 1987), 1.
28. Margaret Tuttle Sprout, "Mahan: Evangelist of Seapower," as reprinted in George Edward Thibault, ed., *The Art and Practice of Military Strategy* (Washington, DC: National Defense University), 1984, 114.
29. Adoption of any particular term in the highly fluid transformation repertoire is risky. Joint interdependence seems to have the "legs" to last. Department of Defense DRAFT Working Paper, Major Combat Operations; Joint Operating Concept, version 1.07 (24 March 2004). The discussion of the concept is taken from Department of the Army White Paper, Serving a Nation at War: A Campaign Quality Army with Joint and Expeditionary Capabilities, (28 April 2004).

CHAPTER 9

AN ANCIENT AND HONORABLE CALLING

"The choice of a line of work," says Professor William Lee Miller, "can be one of the foremost 'moral' choices one makes." It is, Miller continues, "a choice about what it is worthwhile to spend one's life doing."[1] Your decision to undertake a military career of whatever duration, to accept an officer's commission, and to make the officer's oath is particularly weighty. It requires no less than commitment of your life to the service of others, even unto death. In exchange, such service carries with it the benefits and burdens of life as a public official in the world's most successful democracy and membership in an ancient and honorable calling—the profession of arms. Speaking of his own commission, George Washington wrote to a British opponent:

> I cannot conceive of any more honorable [source of officer's rank], than that which flows from the uncorrupted Choice of a brave and free People–The purest Source & original Fountain of all Power.[2]

As an armed forces officer, you accept responsibility both for faithful execution of your office, to include a life of continuous study and application, and the maintenance of an exemplary personal life. This responsibility is owed to the nation, the service, fellow armed forces officers, all those who wear and have worn the nation's uniform in any grade or capacity, as well as those who will come hereafter. The responsibility implies a dual obligation—to protect the Constitution and to pass on the honor of being an armed forces officer in no way diminished by the character of your service.

George Marshall was right: There is a common ground, ethically and morally binding all American military officers, of whatever service, to their particular branch and their fellow armed forces officers. This common ground originates with the common constitutional oath and commission. Indeed, it is the basis of the true professional jointness of the commissioned leaders of all the armed forces.

Logically, it would be as true to say that all officers are commissioned into the Armed Forces of the United States, with service in a particular department, as it is to continue to follow the traditional form of commissioning them into the separate departments and binding them by a common oath and commission. In that sense, all officers are joint officers who happen to be on the establishment of their particular service. It is the common moral obligation that unites the separate service cultures into one fabric—*E pluribus unum.*

As an officer, you must be a warrior, a leader of character, an unwavering defender of the Constitution, a servant of the nation, and an exemplar and champion of its ideals.

The essence of the warrior is an unconquerable will to win, to prevail in the face of all opposition and difficulty. Great flexibility and courage are required of very junior officers in today's operating environment that the Marine Corps calls "the three block war"—subunits of the same formation performing humanitarian assistance, stability, and combat operations within three city blocks.[3] Likewise, great flexibility is required of junior officers of the Coast Guard, commanding small patrol boats and isolated stations at home and abroad. Operating independently, far from command, they bear responsibility to enforce the laws and will of the nation. Endowed with a clear mandate for on-scene initiative, these men and women bear the responsibility for the success of their mission and well being and conduct of their crew.

It is the warrior spirit that will sustain you in times of hardship and discouragement; that will give you the evident confidence and purpose to rally your troops for one more effort when all their will seems to be waning. According to Field Marshal Sir William Slim,

> When you're in command and things have gone wrong there always comes a pause when your men stop and–they look at you. They don't say anything– they just look at you. It's rather an awful moment for the commander because then he knows that their courage is ebbing, their will is fading, and he's got to pull up out of himself the courage and the will power that will stiffen them again and make them go on.[4]

The warrior ethos is Washington, almost single-handedly sustaining the Revolution by maintaining the will of the Continental army through his indomitable example; going over to the attack at Trenton and Princeton in the depths of the winter of 1776. It is Ulysses Grant at Fort Donelson, his line broken and troops driven back, riding to the front and telling his soldiers, "Fill your cartridge-boxes quick, and get into the line; the enemy is trying to escape, and he must not be permitted to do so."[5] It is Captain Guy V. Henry, lying wounded on the battlefield of the Rose Bud, telling a friend, "It is nothing. For this are we soldiers."[6] It is

Admiral Chester Nimitz, ordering Admiral Raymond Spruance to be governed by the principle of calculated risk before the Battle of Midway, then sending him into battle against a superior Japanese fleet.[7] It is the indomitable spirit of Admiral James Stockdale and Lieutenant Lance Sijan, continuing to resist the nation's enemies in spite of injury, captivity and torture. And, it is the spirit that guided Captain Nathan Self and his platoon of Army Rangers, fighting their way to the top of a mountain called Takur Ghar in Afghanistan to recover a lost comrade, a Navy Seal, rather than leave him behind.[8] Warriors will always place the mission first, will never accept defeat, will never quit, and will never leave a fallen comrade behind. The Code of Conduct will be their guide and standard. "I am an American, fighting in the forces which guard my country and our way of life. I am prepared to give my life in their defense."

American warriors, of course, are not simply expected to win. They are expected to win constrained by values important to the American people. This is increasingly important as the actions of Soldiers become immediately visible to the world through instantaneous communications. The application of national values has changed over time, depending, among other things, on the nature of the war and the value of its object to the American people. At a minimum, the American armed forces are expected to fight according to the principles of "Just War" enshrined in international conventions to which the nation is a party. Violation of these rules, however inconvenient or dangerous to one's self or one's unit, is contrary to the national laws of war and indicative of a failure of professional discipline as well as morality. When the armed forces are functioning properly, such violations can be expected to be prosecuted energetically.

The officer owes his subordinates leadership. Captain Daniel Glade, seriously wounded in Iraq and hospitalized at the time at Walter Reed General Hospital, put it this way when asked what he would tell new lieutenants about the responsibilities of commanding troops in battle:

> Tell them that they have to be the unit's leader or commander. To do that you cannot be one of the troops. They do not need another buddy. They need a leader and expect you will step up to that. Be demanding on standards and tough minded in the way you decide and conduct yourself. Care for your troops but be a leader.[9]

The officer, as a leader of character, is responsible to protect his subordinates from the dehumanization that naturally follows descent into the maelstrom of war. The officer must stand above the chaos and travail and guard his or her people's humanity when it is most sorely tried. To do that you must be very secure in the values you stand for and revere, in accordance with the special trust and confidence the president and the nation have reposed in your patriotism, valor, fidelity, and abilities.

As an officer, you are expected to be a leader of character in peace as well as war. Officers are creatures of the law, acting under authority of the president as constitutional commander in chief, according to the laws and regulations laid down by Congress. As a public figure entrusted with the means of war and authority over the lives of fellow citizens, officers' conduct must conform at all times to the highest standards of respect, honor, duty, service, integrity, excellence, courage, commitment, and loyalty. To do less undermines the credit of your service, as well as the professional standing of the corps of American armed forces officers as public trustees of the nation's welfare and security.

The core of the officer's oath is support and defense of the Constitution, while bearing to it, true faith and allegiance. This support and defense is provided by well and faithfully discharging the duties of the office. Support and defense of the Constitution requires, first of all, personal subordination to the civil officials established by the Constitution and the Congress to hold ultimate command on behalf of the American people. By their oaths, armed forces officers are co-opted for the duration of their commission to support, even with their lives, the legal decisions of their civilian leaders, even when they believe they are ill-founded or ill-advised. As Army Chief of Staff General Matthew Ridgway told his subordinates:

> The professional military man has three primary responsibilities:
>
> First, to give his honest, fearless, objective, professional, military opinion of what he needs to do the job given him.
>
> Next, if what he is given is less than the minimum he regards as essential, to give his superiors an honest, fearless, objective opinion of the consequences.
>
> Finally, he has the duty, whatever the final decision, to do the utmost with whatever he is furnished.[10]

Whatever the historical record, it is difficult to see how true faith and allegiance to the Constitution permits the officer in uniform to lobby in opposition to policy decisions with which they are not in agreement. At the same time, it hardly permits of withholding honestly held professional views from constitutionally empowered authorities when called upon to provide them.

The armed forces exist to serve the nation. Broadly speaking, the service we provide is national defense. This service demands unconditional commitment and unlimited liability. Armed forces officers stand in relation to the nation and its government not just as creatures of law but as members of a set of specialist professions, permitted substantial collective control over their own recruitment, training, and performance in exchange for reliability both in the quality of their conduct and effectiveness of their practice. This relationship imposes collective obligations to create new knowledge and to enforce high standards of conduct and performance on the membership of the armed forces and, particularly, on the established leadership—the officer corps.

Armed forces officers must continuously assess their technical skills and upgrade them by study and practice. You must be imaginative, adaptive, and able to respond quickly to new circumstances and threats. You must be self-confident enough in your own skills and abilities to assume responsibility for immediate action out of sight and control of your superiors. You must be self-aware, self-reflective, and self-critical. The American people entrust their sons and daughters to your care. Competence in every aspect of the profession of arms is a moral obligation.

You will not always find the conduct of your fellow professionals to be up to standard. As a member of a profession you will have an obligation to do something to address perceived failures, by questioning, by encouraging, and in egregious cases, by being willing to act. The standard is always what is good for the nation, not what is good in the short term for the profession. Narrow loyalty to the latter can lead to individual and collective deceptions that, in the end, are corrosive of the honor of the profession and all its members. What is good for America is always good for the armed forces.

The armed forces officer carries on an enduring tradition of citizen service to the nation. Your conduct must honor the ideals and principles enshrined in the Declaration of Independence: that all men are created equal, that they are endowed by their Creator with certain unalienable Rights, that among these are Life, Liberty, and the pursuit of Happiness. The officer's demonstrated character, marked by integrity, courage, capability, and commitment, must be such that he or she is worth following into harm's way even at risk of life and limb. The officer as a public figure must model values of a higher standard than those observed by the popular culture, and they must do so without succumbing to the conceit of believing they are better than their masters.

Only when the military articulates and lives up to its highest values can it retain the nobility of the profession of arms. Only when it retains a proper sense of its role in American democratic life does it retain the trust and respect [George C. Marshall] spoke of. Only a military that daily lives out its values and feels its connection to the citizens is a military that engenders the respect and loyalty of the nation and keeps it from being feared.[11]

You have entered an ancient and honorable calling, a life of discipline, hardship, and danger. It is, therefore, a heroic life, for "one who truly lives under obedience is fully disposed to execute instantly and unhesitatingly whatever is enjoined him [or her], no matter whether it be very hard to do."[12] At the end of your service, your reward will be the satisfaction of knowing that your character, competence, and leadership made a difference in your life and for the lives of your countrymen.

1. William Lee Miller, *Lincoln's Virtues* (New York: Vintage Books, 2003), 92.
2. George Washington to Thomas Gage, 19 August 1775, in *George Washington, George Washington: Writings*, John H. Rhodehamel, ed. (New York: Library of America, 1997), 182.
3. The concept was first articulated by General Charles Krulak before the National Press Club on 10 October 1997. *Vital Speeches of the Day*, 64, no. 5 (15 December 1997): 139-142.
4. Field Marshal Sir William Slim, "Higher Command in War," 1952 Kermit Roosevelt Lecture, audio tape, Combined Arms Research Library, U.S. Army Command and General Staff College, Fort Leavenworth, KS.
5. Quoted in J. F. C. Fuller, *The Generalship of Ulysses S. Grant* (Bloomington, IN: Indiana University Press, 1977), 88.
6. John F. Finerty, *Warpath and Bivouac* (Chicago: Donohue, 1890), 130.
7. Thomas B. Buell, *The Quiet Warrior: A Biography of Admiral Raymond A. Spruance* (Boston, MA: Little Brown, 1974), 123-124.
8. Bradley Graham, "Bravery and Breakdowns in a Ridgetop Battle: 7 Americans Died in Rescue Effort That Revealed Mistakes and Determination," *The Washington Post* (24 May 2002), A1.
9. Notes provided by General (Ret.) Frederick M. Franks, Jr., to the students of MS 497, Battle Command, at the United States Military Academy, West Point on 8 March 2005.
10. Matthew Ridgway, *Soldier: The Memoirs of Matthew B. Ridgway as Told to Harold H. Martin* (New York: Harper, 1956), 346.
11. Martin L. Cook, "Moral Foundations of Military Service," *Parameters* 30, no. 1 (Spring, 2000): 117-129, on-line, Internet, 23 May 2004, available from: http://carlisle-www.army.mil/usawc/Parameters/00spring/cook.htm.
12. Jules J. Toner, S. J., quoted in Chris Lowney, *Heroic Leadership: Best Practices From a 450-year-old Company that Changed the World* (Chicago: Loyola Press, 2003), 49.

APPENDIX 1

FOUNDING DOCUMENTS

U.S. NATIONAL ARCHIVES & RECORDS ADMINISTRATION

www.archives.gov — April 2, 2004

The Declaration of Independence: A Transcription

IN CONGRESS, July 4, 1776.

The unanimous Declaration of the thirteen united States of America,

When in the Course of human events, it becomes necessary for one people to dissolve the political bands which have connected them with another, and to assume among the powers of the earth, the separate and equal station to which the Laws of Nature and of Nature's God entitle them, a decent respect to the opinions of mankind requires that they should declare the causes which impel them to the separation.

We hold these truths to be self-evident, that all men are created equal, that they are endowed by their Creator with certain unalienable Rights, that among these are Life, Liberty and the pursuit of Happiness.—That to secure these rights, Governments are instituted among Men, deriving their just powers from the consent of the governed, —That whenever any Form of Government becomes destructive of these ends, it is the Right of the People to alter or to abolish it, and to institute new Government, laying its foundation on such principles and organizing its powers in such form, as to them shall seem most likely to effect their Safety and Happiness. Prudence, indeed, will dictate that Governments long established should not be changed for light and transient causes; and accordingly all experience hath shewn, that mankind are more disposed to suffer, while evils are sufferable, than to right themselves by abolishing the forms to which they are accustomed. But when a long train of abuses and usurpations, pursuing invariably the same Object evinces a design to reduce them under absolute Despotism, it is their right, it is their duty, to throw off such Government, and to provide new Guards for their future security.—Such has been the patient sufferance of these Colonies; and such is now the necessity which constrains them to alter their former Systems of Government. The history of the present King of Great Britain is a history of repeated injuries and usurpations, all having in direct object the establishment of an absolute Tyranny over these States. To prove this, let Facts be submitted to a candid world.

He has refused his Assent to Laws, the most wholesome and necessary for the public good.

He has forbidden his Governors to pass Laws of immediate and pressing importance, unless suspended in their operation till his Assent should be obtained; and when so suspended, he has utterly neglected to attend to them.

He has refused to pass other Laws for the accommodation of large districts of people, unless those people would relinquish the right of Representation in the Legislature, a right inestimable to them and formidable to tyrants only.

He has called together legislative bodies at places unusual, uncomfortable, and distant from the depository of their public Records, for the sole purpose of fatiguing them into compliance with his measures.

He has dissolved Representative Houses repeatedly, for opposing with manly firmness his invasions on the rights of the people.

He has refused for a long time, after such dissolutions, to cause others to be elected; whereby the Legislative powers, incapable of Annihilation, have returned to the People at large for their exercise; the State remaining in the mean time exposed to all the dangers of invasion from without, and convulsions within.

He has endeavoured to prevent the population of these States; for that purpose obstructing the Laws for Naturalization of Foreigners; refusing to pass others to encourage their migrations hither, and raising the conditions of new Appropriations of Lands.

He has obstructed the Administration of Justice, by refusing his Assent to Laws for establishing Judiciary powers.

He has made Judges dependent on his Will alone, for the tenure of their offices, and the amount and payment of their salaries.

He has erected a multitude of New Offices, and sent hither swarms of Officers to harrass our people, and eat out their substance.

He has kept among us, in times of peace, Standing Armies without the Consent of our legislatures.

He has affected to render the Military independent of and superior to the Civil power.

He has combined with others to subject us to a jurisdiction foreign to our constitution, and unacknowledged by our laws; giving his Assent to their Acts of pretended Legislation:

For Quartering large bodies of armed troops among us:

For protecting them, by a mock Trial, from punishment for any Murders which they should commit on the Inhabitants of these States:

For cutting off our Trade with all parts of the world:

For imposing Taxes on us without our Consent:

For depriving us in many cases, of the benefits of Trial by Jury:

For transporting us beyond Seas to be tried for pretended offences

For abolishing the free System of English Laws in a neighbouring Province, establishing therein an Arbitrary government, and enlarging its Boundaries so as to render it at once an example and fit instrument for introducing the same absolute rule into these Colonies:

For taking away our Charters, abolishing our most valuable Laws, and altering fundamentally the Forms of our Governments:

For suspending our own Legislatures, and declaring themselves invested with power to legislate for us in all cases whatsoever.

He has abdicated Government here, by declaring us out of his Protection and waging War against us.

He has plundered our seas, ravaged our Coasts, burnt our towns, and destroyed the lives of our people.

He is at this time transporting large Armies of foreign Mercenaries to compleat the works of death, desolation and tyranny, already begun with circumstances of Cruelty & perfidy scarcely paralleled in the most barbarous ages, and totally unworthy the Head of a civilized nation.

He has constrained our fellow Citizens taken Captive on the high Seas to bear Arms against their Country, to become the executioners of their friends and Brethren, or to fall themselves by their Hands.

He has excited domestic insurrections amongst us, and has endeavoured to bring on the inhabitants of our frontiers, the merciless Indian Savages, whose known rule of warfare, is an undistinguished destruction of all ages, sexes and conditions.

In every stage of these Oppressions We have Petitioned for Redress in the most humble terms: Our repeated Petitions have been answered only by repeated injury. A Prince whose character is thus marked by every act which may define a Tyrant, is unfit to be the ruler of a free people.

Nor have We been wanting in attentions to our Brittish brethren. We have warned them from time to time of attempts by their legislature to extend an unwarrantable jurisdiction over us. We have reminded them of the circumstances of our emigration and settlement here. We have appealed to their native justice and magnanimity, and we have conjured them by the ties of our common kindred to disavow these usurpations, which, would inevitably interrupt our connections and correspondence. They too have been deaf to the voice of justice and of consanguinity. We must, therefore, acquiesce in the necessity, which denounces our Separation, and hold them, as we hold the rest of mankind, Enemies in War, in Peace Friends.

We, therefore, the Representatives of the united States of America, in General Congress, Assembled, appealing to the Supreme Judge of the world for the rectitude of our intentions, do, in the Name, and by Authority of the good People of these Colonies, solemnly publish and declare, That these United Colonies are, and of Right ought to be Free and Independent States; that they are Absolved from all Allegiance to the British Crown, and that all political connection between them and the State of Great Britain, is and ought to be totally dissolved; and that as Free and Independent States, they have full Power to levy War, conclude Peace, contract Alliances, establish Commerce, and to do all other Acts and Things which Independent States may of right do. And for the support of this Declaration, with a firm reliance on the protection of divine Providence, we mutually pledge to each other our Lives, our Fortunes and our sacred Honor.

The 56 signatures on the Declaration appear in the positions indicated:

Column 1
  Georgia:
    Button Gwinnett
    Lyman Hall
    George Walton

Column 2
  North Carolina:
    William Hooper
    Joseph Hewes
    John Penn
  South Carolina:
    Edward Rutledge
    Thomas Heyward, Jr.
    Thomas Lynch, Jr.
    Arthur Middleton

Column 3
  Massachusetts:
    John Hancock

Maryland:
Samuel Chase
William Paca
Thomas Stone
Charles Carroll of Carrollton
Virginia:
George Wythe
Richard Henry Lee
Thomas Jefferson
Benjamin Harrison
Thomas Nelson, Jr.
Francis Lightfoot Lee
Carter Braxton

Column 4
Pennsylvania:
Robert Morris
Benjamin Rush
Benjamin Franklin
John Morton
George Clymer
James Smith
George Taylor
James Wilson
George Ross
Delaware:
Caesar Rodney
George Read
Thomas McKean

Column 5
New York:
William Floyd
Philip Livingston
Francis Lewis
Lewis Morris
New Jersey:
Richard Stockton
John Witherspoon
Francis Hopkinson
John Hart
Abraham Clark

Column 6

New Hampshire:
Josiah Bartlett
William Whipple

Massachusetts:
Samuel Adams
John Adams
Robert Treat Paine
Elbridge Gerry

Rhode Island:
Stephen Hopkins
William Ellery

Connecticut:
Roger Sherman
Samuel Huntington
William Williams
Oliver Wolcott

New Hampshire:
Matthew Thornton

URL:
http://www.archives.gov/national_archives_experience/declaration_transcript.html

---

U.S. National Archives & Records Administration
700 Pennsylvania Avenue NW, Washington, DC 20408 • 1-86-NARA-NARA • 1-866-272-6272

www.archives.gov   April 2, 2004

The Constitution of the United States: A Transcription

Note: The following text is a transcription of the Constitution in its original form.

Items that are underlined have since been amended or superseded.

We the People of the United States, in Order to form a more perfect Union, establish Justice, insure domestic Tranquility, provide for the common defense, promote the general Welfare, and secure the Blessings of Liberty to ourselves and our Posterity, do ordain and establish this Constitution for the United States of America.

Article. I.

Section. 1.

All legislative Powers herein granted shall be vested in a Congress of the United States, which shall consist of a Senate and House of Representatives.

Section. 2.

The House of Representatives shall be composed of Members chosen every second Year by the People of the several States, and the Electors in each State shall have the Qualifications requisite for Electors of the most numerous Branch of the State Legislature.

No Person shall be a Representative who shall not have attained to the Age of twenty five Years, and been seven Years a Citizen of the United States, and who shall not, when elected, be an Inhabitant of that State in which he shall be chosen.

Representatives and direct Taxes shall be apportioned among the several States which may be included within this Union, according to their respective Numbers, which shall be determined by adding to the whole Number of free Persons, including those bound to Service for a Term of Years, and excluding Indians not taxed, three fifths of all other Persons. The actual Enumeration shall be made within three Years after the first Meeting of the Congress of the United States, and within every subsequent Term of ten Years, in such Manner as they shall by Law direct. The Number of Representatives shall not exceed one for every thirty Thousand, but each State shall have at Least one Representative; and until such enumeration shall be made, the State of New Hampshire shall be entitled to chuse three, Massachusetts eight, Rhode-Island and Providence Plantations one, Connecticut five, New-York six, New Jersey four, Pennsylvania eight, Delaware one, Maryland six, Virginia ten, North Carolina five, South Carolina five, and Georgia three.

When vacancies happen in the Representation from any State, the Executive Authority thereof shall issue Writs of Election to fill such Vacancies.

The House of Representatives shall chuse their Speaker and other Officers; and shall have the sole Power of Impeachment.

Section. 3.

The Senate of the United States shall be composed of two Senators from each State, chosen by the Legislature thereof for six Years; and each Senator shall have one Vote.

Immediately after they shall be assembled in Consequence of the first Election, they shall be divided as equally as may be into three Classes. The Seats of the Senators of the first Class shall be vacated at the Expiration of the second Year, of the second Class at the Expiration of the fourth Year, and of the third Class at the Expiration of the sixth Year, so that one third may be chosen every second Year; and if Vacancies happen by Resignation, or otherwise, during the Recess of the Legislature of any State, the Executive thereof may make temporary Appointments until the next Meeting of the Legislature, which shall then fill such Vacancies.

No Person shall be a Senator who shall not have attained to the Age of thirty Years, and been nine Years a Citizen of the United States, and who shall not, when elected, be an Inhabitant of that State for which he shall be chosen.

The Vice President of the United States shall be President of the Senate, but shall have no Vote, unless they be equally divided.

The Senate shall chuse their other Officers, and also a President pro tempore, in the Absence of the Vice President, or when he shall exercise the Office of President of the United States.

The Senate shall have the sole Power to try all Impeachments. When sitting for that Purpose, they shall be on Oath or Affirmation. When the President of the United States is tried, the Chief Justice shall preside: And no Person shall be convicted without the Concurrence of two thirds of the Members present.

Judgment in Cases of Impeachment shall not extend further than to removal from Office, and disqualification to hold and enjoy any Office of honor, Trust or Profit under the United States: but the Party convicted shall nevertheless be liable and subject to Indictment, Trial, Judgment and Punishment, according to Law.

Section. 4.

The Times, Places and Manner of holding Elections for Senators and Representatives, shall be prescribed in each State by the Legislature thereof; but the Congress may at any time by Law make or alter such Regulations, except as to the Places of chusing Senators.

The Congress shall assemble at least once in every Year, and such Meeting shall be on the first Monday in December, unless they shall by Law appoint a different Day.

Section. 5.

Each House shall be the Judge of the Elections, Returns and Qualifications of its own Members, and a Majority of each shall constitute a Quorum to do Business; but a smaller Number may adjourn from day to day, and may be authorized to compel the Attendance of absent Members, in such Manner, and under such Penalties as each House may provide.

Each House may determine the Rules of its Proceedings, punish its Members for disorderly Behaviour, and, with the Concurrence of two thirds, expel a Member.

Each House shall keep a Journal of its Proceedings, and from time to time publish the same, excepting such Parts as may in their Judgment require Secrecy; and the Yeas and Nays of the Members of either House on any question shall, at the Desire of one fifth of those Present, be entered on the Journal.

Neither House, during the Session of Congress, shall, without the Consent of the other, adjourn for more than three days, nor to any other Place than that in which the two Houses shall be sitting.

Section. 6.

The Senators and Representatives shall receive a Compensation for their Services, to be ascertained by Law, and paid out of the Treasury of the United States. They shall in all Cases, except Treason, Felony and Breach of the Peace, be privileged from Arrest during their Attendance at the Session of their respective Houses, and in going to and returning from the same; and for any Speech or Debate in either House, they shall not be questioned in any other Place.

No Senator or Representative shall, during the Time for which he was elected, be appointed to any civil Office under the Authority of the United States, which shall have been created, or the Emoluments whereof shall have been encreased during such time; and no Person holding any Office under the United States, shall be a Member of either House during his Continuance in Office.

Section. 7.

All Bills for raising Revenue shall originate in the House of Representatives; but the Senate may propose or concur with Amendments as on other Bills.

Every Bill which shall have passed the House of Representatives and the Senate, shall, before it become a Law, be presented to the President of the United States: If he approve he shall sign it, but if not he shall return it, with his Objections to that House in which it shall have originated, who shall enter the Objections at large on their Journal, and proceed to reconsider it.If after such Reconsideration two thirds of that House shall agree to pass the Bill, it shall be sent, together with the Objections, to the other House, by which it shall likewise be reconsidered, and if approved by two thirds of that House, it shall become a Law. But in all such Cases the Votes of both Houses shall be determined by yeas and Nays, and the Names of the Persons voting for and against the Bill shall be entered on the Journal of each House respectively. If any Bill shall not be returned by the President within ten Days (Sundays excepted) after it shall have been presented to him, the Same shall be a Law, in like Manner as if he had signed it, unless the Congress by their Adjournment prevent its Return, in which Case it shall not be a Law.

Every Order, Resolution, or Vote to which the Concurrence of the Senate and House of Representatives may be necessary (except on a question of Adjournment) shall be presented to the President of the United States; and before the Same shall take Effect, shall be approved by him, or being disapproved by him, shall be repassed by two thirds of the Senate and House of Representatives, according to the Rules and Limitations prescribed in the Case of a Bill.

Section. 8.

The Congress shall have Power To lay and collect Taxes, Duties, Imposts and Excises, to pay the Debts and provide for the common Defence and general Welfare of the United States; but all Duties, Imposts and Excises shall be uniform throughout the United States;

To borrow Money on the credit of the United States;

To regulate Commerce with foreign Nations, and among the several States, and with the Indian Tribes;

To establish an uniform Rule of Naturalization, and uniform Laws on the subject of Bankruptcies throughout the United States;

To coin Money, regulate the Value thereof, and of foreign Coin, and fix the Standard of Weights and Measures;

To provide for the Punishment of counterfeiting the Securities and current Coin of the United States;

To establish Post Offices and post Roads;

To promote the Progress of Science and useful Arts, by securing for limited Times to Authors and Inventors the exclusive Right to their respective Writings and Discoveries;

To constitute Tribunals inferior to the supreme Court;

To define and punish Piracies and Felonies committed on the high Seas, and Offences against the Law of Nations;

To declare War, grant Letters of Marque and Reprisal, and make Rules concerning Captures on Land and Water;

To raise and support Armies, but no Appropriation of Money to that Use shall be for a longer Term than two Years;

To provide and maintain a Navy;

To make Rules for the Government and Regulation of the land and naval Forces;

To provide for calling forth the Militia to execute the Laws of the Union, suppress Insurrections and repel Invasions;

To provide for organizing, arming, and disciplining, the Militia, and for governing such Part of them as may be employed in the Service of the United States, reserving to the States respectively, the Appointment of the Officers, and the Authority of training the Militia according to the discipline prescribed by Congress;

To exercise exclusive Legislation in all Cases whatsoever, over such District (not exceeding ten Miles square) as may, by Cession of particular States, and the Acceptance of Congress, become the Seat of the Government of the United States, and to exercise like Authority over all Places purchased by the Consent of the Legislature of the State in which the Same shall be, for the Erection of Forts, Magazines, Arsenals, dock-Yards, and other needful Buildings;—And

To make all Laws which shall be necessary and proper for carrying into Execution the foregoing Powers, and all other Powers vested by this Constitution in the Government of the United States, or in any Department or Officer thereof.

Section. 9.

The Migration or Importation of such Persons as any of the States now existing shall think proper to admit, shall not be prohibited by the Congress prior to the Year one thousand eight hundred and eight, but a Tax or duty may be imposed on such Importation, not exceeding ten dollars for each Person.

The Privilege of the Writ of Habeas Corpus shall not be suspended, unless when in Cases of Rebellion or Invasion the public Safety may require it.

No Bill of Attainder or ex post facto Law shall be passed.

No Capitation, or other direct, Tax shall be laid, unless in Proportion to the Census or enumeration herein before directed to be taken.

No Tax or Duty shall be laid on Articles exported from any State.

No Preference shall be given by any Regulation of Commerce or Revenue to the Ports of one State over those of another; nor shall Vessels bound to, or from, one State, be obliged to enter, clear, or pay Duties in another.

No Money shall be drawn from the Treasury, but in Consequence of

Appropriations made by Law; and a regular Statement and Account of the Receipts and Expenditures of all public Money shall be published from time to time.

No Title of Nobility shall be granted by the United States: And no Person holding any Office of Profit or Trust under them, shall, without the Consent of the Congress, accept of any present, Emolument, Office, or Title, of any kind whatever, from any King, Prince, or foreign State.

Section. 10.

No State shall enter into any Treaty, Alliance, or Confederation; grant Letters of Marque and Reprisal; coin Money; emit Bills of Credit; make any Thing but gold and silver Coin a Tender in Payment of Debts; pass any Bill of Attainder, ex post facto Law, or Law impairing the Obligation of Contracts, or grant any Title of Nobility.

No State shall, without the Consent of the Congress, lay any Imposts or Duties on Imports or Exports, except what may be absolutely necessary for executing it's inspection Laws: and the net Produce of all Duties and Imposts, laid by any State on Imports or Exports, shall be for the Use of the Treasury of the United States; and all such Laws shall be subject to the Revision and Controul of the Congress.

No State shall, without the Consent of Congress, lay any Duty of Tonnage, keep Troops, or Ships of War in time of Peace, enter into any Agreement or Compact with another State, or with a foreign Power, or engage in War, unless actually invaded, or in such imminent Danger as will not admit of delay.

Article. II.

Section. 1.

The executive Power shall be vested in a President of the United States of America. He shall hold his Office during the Term of four Years, and, together with the Vice President, chosen for the same Term, be elected, as follows:

Each State shall appoint, in such Manner as the Legislature thereof may direct, a Number of Electors, equal to the whole Number of Senators and Representatives to which the State may be entitled in the Congress: but no Senator or Representative, or Person holding an Office of Trust or Profit under the United States, shall be appointed an Elector.

The Electors shall meet in their respective States, and vote by Ballot for two Persons, of whom one at least shall not be an Inhabitant of the same State with themselves. And they shall make a List of all the Persons voted for, and of the

Number of Votes for each; which List they shall sign and certify, and transmit sealed to the Seat of the Government of the United States, directed to the President of the Senate. The President of the Senate shall, in the Presence of the Senate and House of Representatives, open all the Certificates, and the Votes shall then be counted. The Person having the greatest Number of Votes shall be the President, if such Number be a Majority of the whole Number of Electors appointed; and if there be more than one who have such Majority, and have an equal Number of Votes, then the House of Representatives shall immediately chuse by Ballot one of them for President; and if no Person have a Majority, then from the five highest on the List the said House shall in like Manner chuse the President. But in chusing the President, the Votes shall be taken by States, the Representation from each State having one Vote; A quorum for this purpose shall consist of a Member or Members from two thirds of the States, and a Majority of all the States shall be necessary to a Choice. In every Case, after the Choice of the President, the Person having the greatest Number of Votes of the Electors shall be the Vice President. But if there should remain two or more who have equal Votes, the Senate shall chuse from them by Ballot the Vice President.

The Congress may determine the Time of chusing the Electors, and the Day on which they shall give their Votes; which Day shall be the same throughout the United States.

No Person except a natural born Citizen, or a Citizen of the United States, at the time of the Adoption of this Constitution, shall be eligible to the Office of President; neither shall any Person be eligible to that Office who shall not have attained to the Age of thirty five Years, and been fourteen Years a Resident within the United States.

In Case of the Removal of the President from Office, or of his Death, Resignation, or Inability to discharge the Powers and Duties of the said Office, the Same shall devolve on the Vice President, and the Congress may by Law provide for the Case of Removal, Death, Resignation or Inability, both of the President and Vice President, declaring what Officer shall then act as President, and such Officer shall act accordingly, until the Disability be removed, or a President shall be elected.

The President shall, at stated Times, receive for his Services, a Compensation, which shall neither be increased nor diminished during the Period for which he shall have been elected, and he shall not receive within that Period any other Emolument from the United States, or any of them.

Before he enter on the Execution of his Office, he shall take the following Oath or Affirmation:—"I do solemnly swear (or affirm) that I will faithfully execute the Office of President of the United States, and will to the best of my Ability, preserve, protect and defend the Constitution of the United States."

Section. 2.

The President shall be Commander in Chief of the Army and Navy of the United States, and of the Militia of the several States, when called into the actual Service of the United States; he may require the Opinion, in writing, of the principal Officer in each of the executive Departments, upon any Subject relating to the Duties of their respective Offices, and he shall have Power to grant Reprieves and Pardons for Offences against the United States, except in Cases of Impeachment.

He shall have Power, by and with the Advice and Consent of the Senate, to make Treaties, provided two thirds of the Senators present concur; and he shall nominate, and by and with the Advice and Consent of the Senate, shall appoint Ambassadors, other public Ministers and Consuls, Judges of the supreme Court, and all other Officers of the United States, whose Appointments are not herein otherwise provided for, and which shall be established by Law: but the Congress may by Law vest the Appointment of such inferior Officers, as they think proper, in the President alone, in the Courts of Law, or in the Heads of Departments.

The President shall have Power to fill up all Vacancies that may happen during the Recess of the Senate, by granting Commissions which shall expire at the End of their next Session.

Section. 3.

He shall from time to time give to the Congress Information of the State of the Union, and recommend to their Consideration such Measures as he shall judge necessary and expedient; he may, on extraordinary Occasions, convene both Houses, or either of them, and in Case of Disagreement between them, with Respect to the Time of Adjournment, he may adjourn them to such Time as he shall think proper; he shall receive Ambassadors and other public Ministers; he shall take Care that the Laws be faithfully executed, and shall Commission all the Officers of the United States.

Section. 4.

The President, Vice President and all civil Officers of the United States, shall be removed from Office on Impeachment for, and Conviction of, Treason, Bribery, or other high Crimes and Misdemeanors.

Article III.

Section. 1.

The judicial Power of the United States shall be vested in one supreme Court, and in such inferior Courts as the Congress may from time to time ordain

---

and establish. The Judges, both of the supreme and inferior Courts, shall hold their Offices during good Behaviour, and shall, at stated Times, receive for their Services a Compensation, which shall not be diminished during their Continuance in Office.

Section. 2.

The judicial Power shall extend to all Cases, in Law and Equity, arising under this Constitution, the Laws of the United States, and Treaties made, or which shall be made, under their Authority;—to all Cases affecting Ambassadors, other public Ministers and Consuls;—to all Cases of admiralty and maritime Jurisdiction;—to Controversies to which the United States shall be a Party;—to Controversies between two or more States;—between a State and Citizens of another State;—between Citizens of different States;—between Citizens of the same State claiming Lands under Grants of different States, and between a State, or the Citizens thereof, and foreign States, Citizens or Subjects.

In all Cases affecting Ambassadors, other public Ministers and Consuls, and those in which a State shall be Party, the supreme Court shall have original Jurisdiction. In all the other Cases before mentioned, the supreme Court shall have appellate Jurisdiction, both as to Law and Fact, with such Exceptions, and under such Regulations as the Congress shall make.

The Trial of all Crimes, except in Cases of Impeachment, shall be by Jury; and such Trial shall be held in the State where the said Crimes shall have been committed; but when not committed within any State, the Trial shall be at such Place or Places as the Congress may by Law have directed.

Section. 3.

Treason against the United States, shall consist only in levying War against them, or in adhering to their Enemies, giving them Aid and Comfort. No Person shall be convicted of Treason unless on the Testimony of two Witnesses to the same overt Act, or on Confession in open Court.

The Congress shall have Power to declare the Punishment of Treason, but no Attainder of Treason shall work Corruption of Blood, or Forfeiture except during the Life of the Person attainted.

Article. IV.

Section. 1.

Full Faith and Credit shall be given in each State to the public Acts, Records, and judicial Proceedings of every other State. And the Congress may by general Laws prescribe the Manner in which such Acts, Records and Proceedings shall be proved, and the Effect thereof.

Section. 2.

The Citizens of each State shall be entitled to all Privileges and Immunities of Citizens in the several States.

A Person charged in any State with Treason, Felony, or other Crime, who shall flee from Justice, and be found in another State, shall on Demand of the executive Authority of the State from which he fled, be delivered up, to be removed to the State having Jurisdiction of the Crime.

No Person held to Service or Labour in one State, under the Laws thereof, escaping into another, shall, in Consequence of any Law or Regulation therein, be discharged from such Service or Labour, but shall be delivered up on Claim of the Party to whom such Service or Labour may be due.

Section. 3.

New States may be admitted by the Congress into this Union; but no new State shall be formed or erected within the Jurisdiction of any other State; nor any State be formed by the Junction of two or more States, or Parts of States, without the Consent of the Legislatures of the States concerned as well as of the Congress.

The Congress shall have Power to dispose of and make all needful Rules and Regulations respecting the Territory or other Property belonging to the United States; and nothing in this Constitution shall be so construed as to Prejudice any Claims of the United States, or of any particular State.

Section. 4.

The United States shall guarantee to every State in this Union a Republican Form of Government, and shall protect each of them against Invasion; and on Application of the Legislature, or of the Executive (when the Legislature cannot be convened), against domestic Violence.

Article. V.

The Congress, whenever two thirds of both Houses shall deem it necessary, shall propose Amendments to this Constitution, or, on the Application of the Legislatures of two thirds of the several States, shall call a Convention for proposing Amendments, which, in either Case, shall be valid to all Intents and Purposes, as Part of this Constitution, when ratified by the Legislatures of three fourths of the several States, or by Conventions in three fourths thereof, as the one or the other Mode of Ratification may be proposed by the Congress; Provided that no Amendment which may be made prior to the Year One thousand eight hundred and eight shall in any Manner affect the first and fourth Clauses in the

Ninth Section of the first Article; and that no State, without its Consent, shall be deprived of its equal Suffrage in the Senate.

Article. VI.

All Debts contracted and Engagements entered into, before the Adoption of this Constitution, shall be as valid against the United States under this Constitution, as under the Confederation.

This Constitution, and the Laws of the United States which shall be made in Pursuance thereof; and all Treaties made, or which shall be made, under the Authority of the United States, shall be the supreme Law of the Land; and the Judges in every State shall be bound thereby, any Thing in the Constitution or Laws of any State to the Contrary notwithstanding.

The Senators and Representatives before mentioned, and the Members of the several State Legislatures, and all executive and judicial Officers, both of the United States and of the several States, shall be bound by Oath or Affirmation, to support this Constitution; but no religious Test shall ever be required as a Qualification to any Office or public Trust under the United States.

Article. VII.

The Ratification of the Conventions of nine States, shall be sufficient for the Establishment of this Constitution between the States so ratifying the Same.

The Word, "the," being interlined between the seventh and eighth Lines of the first Page, the Word "Thirty" being partly written on an Erazure in the fifteenth Line of the first Page, The Words "is tried" being interlined between the thirty second and thirty third Lines of the first Page and the Word "the" being interlined between the forty third and forty fourth Lines of the second Page.

Attest William Jackson Secretary

Done in Convention by the Unanimous Consent of the States present the Seventeenth Day of September in the Year of our Lord one thousand seven hundred and Eighty seven and of the Independence of the United States of America the Twelfth In witness whereof We have hereunto subscribed our Names,

G°. Washington
Presidt and deputy from Virginia

Delaware
    Geo: Read

Gunning Bedford jun
John Dickinson
Richard Bassett
Jaco: Broom

Maryland
James McHenry
Dan of St Thos. Jenifer
Danl. Carroll

Virginia
John Blair
James Madison Jr.

North Carolina
Wm. Blount
Richd. Dobbs Spaight
Hu Williamson

South Carolina
J. Rutledge
Charles Cotesworth Pinckney
Charles Pinckney
Pierce Butler

Georgia
William Few
Abr Baldwin

New Hampshire
John Langdon
Nicholas Gilman

Massachusetts
Nathaniel Gorham
Rufus King

Connecticut
Wm. Saml. Johnson
Roger Sherman

New York
Alexander Hamilton

New Jersey
Wil: Livingston
David Brearley
Wm. Paterson
Jona: Dayton

Pennsylvania
B Franklin
Thomas Mifflin
Robt. Morris
Geo. Clymer
Thos. FitzSimons
Jared Ingersoll
James Wilson
Gouv Morris

For biographies of the nonsigning delegates to the Constitutional Convention, see the Founding Fathers page.

URL:
http://www.archives.gov/national_archives_experience/constitution_ transcript.html.

U.S. National Archives & Records Administration
700 Pennsylvania Avenue NW, Washington, DC 20408 • 1-86-NARA-NARA • 1-866-272-6272

The Bill of Rights: A Transcription

Note: The following text is a transcription of the first ten amendments to the Constitution in their original form. These amendments were ratified December 15, 1791, and form what is known as the "Bill of Rights."

Amendment I

Congress shall make no law respecting an establishment of religion, or prohibiting the free exercise thereof; or abridging the freedom of speech, or of the press; or the right of the people peaceably to assemble, and to petition the Government for a redress of grievances.

Amendment II

A well regulated Militia, being necessary to the security of a free State, the right of the people to keep and bear Arms, shall not be infringed.

Amendment III

No Soldier shall, in time of peace be quartered in any house, without the consent of the Owner, nor in time of war, but in a manner to be prescribed by law.

Amendment IV

The right of the people to be secure in their persons, houses, papers, and effects, against unreasonable searches and seizures, shall not be violated, and no Warrants shall issue, but upon probable cause, supported by Oath or affirmation, and particularly describing the place to be searched, and the persons or things to be seized.

Amendment V

No person shall be held to answer for a capital, or otherwise infamous crime, unless on a presentment or indictment of a Grand Jury, except in cases arising in the land or naval forces, or in the Militia, when in actual service in time of War or public danger; nor shall any person be subject for the same offence to be twice put in jeopardy of life or limb; nor shall be compelled in any criminal case to be a witness against himself, nor be deprived of life, liberty, or property, without due process of law; nor shall private property be taken for public use, without just compensation.

Amendment VI

In all criminal prosecutions, the accused shall enjoy the right to a speedy and public trial, by an impartial jury of the State and district wherein the crime shall have been committed, which district shall have been previously ascertained by law, and to be informed of the nature and cause of the accusation; to be confronted with the witnesses against him; to have compulsory process for obtaining witnesses in his favor, and to have the Assistance of Counsel for his defence.

Amendment VII

In Suits at common law, where the value in controversy shall exceed twenty dollars, the right of trial by jury shall be preserved, and no fact tried by a jury, shall be otherwise reexamined in any Court of the United States, than according to the rules of the common law.

Amendment VIII

Excessive bail shall not be required, nor excessive fines imposed, nor cruel and unusual punishments inflicted.

Amendment IX

The enumeration in the Constitution, of certain rights, shall not be construed to deny or disparage others retained by the people.

Amendment X

The powers not delegated to the United States by the Constitution, nor prohibited by it to the States, are reserved to the States respectively, or to the people.

Note: The capitalization and punctuation in this version is from the enrolle original of the Joint Resolution of Congress proposing the Bill of Rights, which is on permanent display in the Rotunda of the National Archives Building, Washington, D.C.

The Constitution: Amendments 11-27

Constitutional Amendments 1-10 make up what is known as <u>The Bill of Rights</u>. Amendments 11-27 are listed below.

AMENDMENT XI

Passed by Congress March 4, 1794. Ratified February 7, 1795.

Note: Article III, section 2, of the Constitution was modified by amendment 11.

The Judicial power of the United States shall not be construed to extend to any suit in law or equity, commenced or prosecuted against one of the United States by Citizens of another State, or by Citizens or Subjects of any Foreign State.

AMENDMENT XII

Passed by Congress December 9, 1803. Ratified June 15, 1804.

Note: A portion of Article II, section 1 of the Constitution was superseded by the 12th amendment.

The Electors shall meet in their respective states and vote by ballot for President and Vice-President, one of whom, at least, shall not be an inhabitant of the same state with themselves; they shall name in their ballots the person voted for as President, and in distinct ballots the person voted for as Vice-President, and they shall make distinct lists of all persons voted for as President, and of all persons voted for as Vice-President, and of the number of votes for each, which lists they shall sign and certify, and transmit sealed to the seat of the government of the United States, directed to the President of the Senate; —the President of the Senate shall, in the presence of the Senate and House of Representatives, open all the certificates and the votes shall then be counted; —The person having the greatest number of votes for President, shall be the President, if such number be a majority of the whole number of Electors appointed; and if no person have such majority, then from the persons having the highest numbers not exceeding three on the list of those voted for as President, the House of Representatives shall choose immediately, by ballot, the President. But in choosing the President, the votes shall be taken by states, the representation from each state having one vote; a quorum for this purpose shall consist of a member or members from two-thirds of the states, and a majority of all the states shall be necessary to a choice. [And if the House of Representatives shall not choose a President whenever the right of choice shall devolve upon them, before the fourth day of March next following, then the Vice-President shall act as President, as in case of the death or other constitutional disability of the President. --]* The person having the greatest number of votes as Vice-President, shall be the Vice-President, if such number be a majority of the whole number of Electors appointed, and if no person have a majority, then from the two highest numbers on the list, the Senate shall choose the Vice-President; a quorum for the purpose shall consist of two-thirds of the whole number of Senators, and a majority of the whole number shall be necessary to a choice. But no person constitutionally ineligible to the office of President shall be eligible to that of Vice-President of the United States.

*Superseded by section 3 of the 20th amendment.

AMENDMENT XIII

Passed by Congress January 31, 1865. Ratified December 6, 1865.

Note: A portion of Article IV, section 2, of the Constitution was superseded by the 13th amendment.

Section 1.
Neither slavery nor involuntary servitude, except as a punishment for crime whereof the party shall have been duly convicted, shall exist within the United States, or any place subject to their jurisdiction.

Section 2.
Congress shall have power to enforce this article by appropriate legislation.

AMENDMENT XIV

Passed by Congress June 13, 1866. Ratified July 9, 1868.

Note: Article I, section 2, of the Constitution was modified by section 2 of the 14th amendment.

Section 1.
All persons born or naturalized in the United States, and subject to the jurisdiction thereof, are citizens of the United States and of the State wherein they

reside. No State shall make or enforce any law which shall abridge the privileges or immunities of citizens of the United States; nor shall any State deprive any person of life, liberty, or property, without due process of law; nor deny to any person within its jurisdiction the equal protection of the laws.

Section 2.

Representatives shall be apportioned among the several States according to their respective numbers, counting the whole number of persons in each State, excluding Indians not taxed. But when the right to vote at any election for the choice of electors for President and Vice-President of the United States, Representatives in Congress, the Executive and Judicial officers of a State, or the members of the Legislature thereof, is denied to any of the male inhabitants of such State, being twenty-one years of age,* and citizens of the United States, or in any way abridged, except for participation in rebellion, or other crime, the basis of representation therein shall be reduced in the proportion which the number of such male citizens shall bear to the whole number of male citizens twenty-one years of age in such State.

Section 3.

No person shall be a Senator or Representative in Congress, or elector of President and Vice-President, or hold any office, civil or military, under the United States, or under any State, who, having previously taken an oath, as a member of Congress, or as an officer of the United States, or as a member of any State legislature, or as an executive or judicial officer of any State, to support the Constitution of the United States, shall have engaged in insurrection or rebellion against the same, or given aid or comfort to the enemies thereof. But Congress may by a vote of two-thirds of each House, remove such disability.

Section 4.

The validity of the public debt of the United States, authorized by law, including debts incurred for payment of pensions and bounties for services in suppressing insurrection or rebellion, shall not be questioned. But neither the United States nor any State shall assume or pay any debt or obligation incurred in aid of insurrection or rebellion against the United States, or any claim for the loss or emancipation of any slave; but all such debts, obligations and claims shall be held illegal and void.

Section 5.

The Congress shall have the power to enforce, by appropriate legislation, the provisions of this article.

Changed by section 1 of the 26th amendment.

AMENDMENT XV

Passed by Congress February 26, 1869. Ratified February 3, 1870.

Section 1.
The right of citizens of the United States to vote shall not be denied or abridged by the United States or by any State on account of race, color, or previous condition of servitude--

Section 2.
The Congress shall have the power to enforce this article by appropriate legislation.

AMENDMENT XVI

Passed by Congress July 2, 1909. Ratified February 3, 1913.

Note: Article I, section 9, of the Constitution was modified by amendment 16.

The Congress shall have power to lay and collect taxes on incomes, from whatever source derived, without apportionment among the several States, and without regard to any census or enumeration.

AMENDMENT XVII

Passed by Congress May 13, 1912. Ratified April 8, 1913.

Note: Article I, section 3, of the Constitution was modified by the 17th amendment.

The Senate of the United States shall be composed of two Senators from each State, elected by the people thereof, for six years; and each Senator shall have one vote. The electors in each State shall have the qualifications requisite for electors of the most numerous branch of the State legislatures.

When vacancies happen in the representation of any State in the Senate, the executive authority of such State shall issue writs of election to fill such vacancies: Provided, That the legislature of any State may empower the executive thereof to make temporary appointments until the people fill the vacancies by election as the legislature may direct.

This amendment shall not be so construed as to affect the election or term of any Senator chosen before it becomes valid as part of the Constitution.

AMENDMENT XVIII

Passed by Congress December 18, 1917. Ratified January 16, 1919. Repealed by amendment 21.

Section 1.
After one year from the ratification of this article the manufacture, sale, or transportation of intoxicating liquors within, the importation thereof into, or the exportation thereof from the United States and all territory subject to the jurisdiction thereof for beverage purposes is hereby prohibited.

Section 2.
The Congress and the several States shall have concurrent power to enforce this article by appropriate legislation.

Section 3.
This article shall be inoperative unless it shall have been ratified as an amendment to the Constitution by the legislatures of the several States, as provided in the Constitution, within seven years from the date of the submission hereof to the States by the Congress.

AMENDMENT XIX

Passed by Congress June 4, 1919. Ratified August 18, 1920.

The right of citizens of the United States to vote shall not be denied or abridged by the United States or by any State on account of sex.

Congress shall have power to enforce this article by appropriate legislation.

AMENDMENT XX

Passed by Congress March 2, 1932. Ratified January 23, 1933.

Note: Article I, section 4, of the Constitution was modified by section 2 of this amendment. In addition, a portion of the 12th amendment was superseded by section 3.

Section 1.
The terms of the President and the Vice President shall end at noon on the 20th day of January, and the terms of Senators and Representatives at noon on the 3d day of January, of the years in which such terms would have ended if this article had not been ratified; and the terms of their successors shall then begin.

Section 2.

The Congress shall assemble at least once in every year, and such meeting shall begin at noon on the 3d day of January, unless they shall by law appoint a different day.

Section 3.

If, at the time fixed for the beginning of the term of the President, the President elect shall have died, the Vice President elect shall become President. If a President shall not have been chosen before the time fixed for the beginning of his term, or if the President elect shall have failed to qualify, then the Vice President elect shall act as President until a President shall have qualified; and the Congress may by law provide for the case wherein neither a President elect nor a Vice President shall have qualified, declaring who shall then act as President, or the manner in which one who is to act shall be selected, and such person shall act accordingly until a President or Vice President shall have qualified.

Section 4.

The Congress may by law provide for the case of the death of any of the persons from whom the House of Representatives may choose a President whenever the right of choice shall have devolved upon them, and for the case of the death of any of the persons from whom the Senate may choose a Vice President whenever the right of choice shall have devolved upon them.

Section 5.

Sections 1 and 2 shall take effect on the 15th day of October following the ratification of this article.

Section 6.

This article shall be inoperative unless it shall have been ratified as an amendment to the Constitution by the legislatures of three-fourths of the several States within seven years from the date of its submission.

AMENDMENT XXI

Passed by Congress February 20, 1933. Ratified December 5, 1933.

Section 1.

The eighteenth article of amendment to the Constitution of the United States is hereby repealed.

Section 2.

The transportation or importation into any State, Territory, or Possession of the United States for delivery or use therein of intoxicating liquors, in violation of the laws thereof, is hereby prohibited.

Section 3.

This article shall be inoperative unless it shall have been ratified as an amendment to the Constitution by conventions in the several States, as provided in the Constitution, within seven years from the date of the submission hereof to the States by the Congress.

AMENDMENT XXII

Passed by Congress March 21, 1947. Ratified February 27, 1951.

Section 1.

No person shall be elected to the office of the President more than twice, and no person who has held the office of President, or acted as President, for more than two years of a term to which some other person was elected President shall be elected to the office of President more than once. But this Article shall not apply to any person holding the office of President when this Article was proposed by Congress, and shall not prevent any person who may be holding the office of President, or acting as President, during the term within which this Article becomes operative from holding the office of President or acting as President during the remainder of such term.

Section 2.

This article shall be inoperative unless it shall have been ratified as an amendment to the Constitution by the legislatures of three-fourths of the several States within seven years from the date of its submission to the States by the Congress.

AMENDMENT XXIII

Passed by Congress June 16, 1960. Ratified March 29, 1961.

Section 1.

The District constituting the seat of Government of the United States shall appoint in such manner as Congress may direct:

A number of electors of President and Vice President equal to the whole number of Senators and Representatives in Congress to which the District would be entitled if it were a State, but in no event more than the least populous State; they shall be in addition to those appointed by the States, but they shall be considered, for the purposes of the election of President and Vice President, to be electors

---

appointed by a State; and they shall meet in the District and perform such duties as provided by the twelfth article of amendment.

Section 2.

The Congress shall have power to enforce this article by appropriate legislation.

AMENDMENT XXIV

Passed by Congress August 27, 1962. Ratified January 23, 1964.

Section 1.

The right of citizens of the United States to vote in any primary or other election for President or Vice President, for electors for President or Vice President, or for Senator or Representative in Congress, shall not be denied or abridged by the United States or any State by reason of failure to pay poll tax or other tax.

Section 2.

The Congress shall have power to enforce this article by appropriate legislation.

AMENDMENT XXV

Passed by Congress July 6, 1965. Ratified February 10, 1967.

Note: Article II, section 1, of the Constitution was affected by the 25th amendment.

Section 1.

In case of the removal of the President from office or of his death or resignation, the Vice President shall become President.

Section 2.

Whenever there is a vacancy in the office of the Vice President, the President shall nominate a Vice President who shall take office upon confirmation by a majority vote of both Houses of Congress.

Section 3.

Whenever the President transmits to the President pro tempore of the Senate and the Speaker of the House of Representatives his written declaration that he is unable to discharge the powers and duties of his office, and until he transmits to them a written declaration to the contrary, such powers and duties shall be discharged by the Vice President as Acting President.

Section 4.

Whenever the Vice President and a majority of either the principal officers of the executive departments or of such other body as Congress may by law provide, transmit to the President pro tempore of the Senate and the Speaker of the House of Representatives their written declaration that the President is unable to discharge the powers and duties of his office, the Vice President shall immediately assume the powers and duties of the office as Acting President.

Thereafter, when the President transmits to the President pro tempore of the Senate and the Speaker of the House of Representatives his written declaration that no inability exists, he shall resume the powers and duties of his office unless the Vice President and a majority of either the principal officers of the executive department or of such other body as Congress may by law provide, transmit within four days to the President pro tempore of the Senate and the Speaker of the House of Representatives their written declaration that the President is unable to discharge the powers and duties of his office. Thereupon Congress shall decide the issue, assembling within forty-eight hours for that purpose if not in session. If the Congress, within twenty-one days after receipt of the latter written declaration, or, if Congress is not in session, within twenty-one days after Congress is required to assemble, determines by two-thirds vote of both

Houses that the President is unable to discharge the powers and duties of his office, the Vice President shall continue to discharge the same as Acting President; otherwise, the President shall resume the powers and duties of his office.

AMENDMENT XXVI

Passed by Congress March 23, 1971. Ratified July 1, 1971.

Note: Amendment 14, section 2, of the Constitution was modified by section 1 of the 26th amendment.

Section 1.

The right of citizens of the United States, who are eighteen years of age or older, to vote shall not be denied or abridged by the United States or by any State on account of age.

Section 2.

The Congress shall have power to enforce this article by appropriate legislation.

AMENDMENT XXVII

Originally proposed Sept. 25, 1789. Ratified May 7, 1992.

No law, varying the compensation for the services of the Senators and Representatives, shall take effect, until an election of representatives shall have inter-
vened.

URL:
http://www.archives.gov/national_archives_experience/charters/
constitution_amendments_11-27.html.

U.S. National Archives & Records Administration
700 Pennsylvania Avenue NW, Washington, DC 20408 • 1-86-NARA-NARA •
1-866-272-6272

APPENDIX 2

AUTHORIZING STATUTES FOR THE ARMED FORCES

The United States Air Force

TITLE 10, Subtitle D, PART I, CHAPTER 807

Sec. 8062. Policy; composition; aircraft authorization

(a) It is the intent of Congress to provide an Air Force that is capable, in conjunction with the other armed forces, of

> **(1)** preserving the peace and security, and providing for the defense, of the United States, the Territories, Commonwealths, and possessions, and any areas occupied by the United States;
>
> **(2)** supporting the national policies;
>
> **(3)** implementing the national objectives; and
>
> **(4)** overcoming any nations responsible for aggressive acts that imperil the peace and security of the United States.

(b) There is a United States Air Force within the Department of the Air Force.

(c) In general, the Air Force includes aviation forces both combat and service not otherwise assigned. It shall be organized, trained, and equipped primarily for prompt and sustained offensive and defensive air operations. It is responsible for the preparation of the air forces necessary for the effective prosecution of war except as otherwise assigned and, in accordance with integrated joint mobilization plans, for the expansion of the peacetime components of the Air Force to meet the needs of war.

(d) The Air Force consists of

    (1) the Regular Air Force, the Air National Guard of the United States, the Air National Guard while in the service of the United States, and the Air Force Reserve;

    (2) all persons appointed or enlisted in, or conscripted into, the Air Force without component; and

    (3) all Air Force units and other Air Force organizations, with their installations and supporting and auxiliary combat, training, administrative, and logistic elements; and all members of the Air Force, including those not assigned to units; necessary to form the basis for a complete and immediate mobilization for the national defense in the event of a national emergency.

(e) Subject to subsection (f) of this section, chapter 831 of this title, and the strength authorized by law pursuant to section 115 of this title, the authorized strength of the Air Force is 70 Regular Air Force groups and such separate Regular Air Force squadrons, reserve groups, and supporting and auxiliary regular and reserve units as required.

(f) There are authorized for the Air Force 24,000 serviceable aircraft or 225,000 airframe tons of serviceable aircraft, whichever the Secretary of the Air Force considers appropriate to carry out this section. This subsection does not apply to guided missiles.

The United States Army

TITLE 10, Subtitle B, PART I, CHAPTER 307.

Sec. 3062. Policy; composition; organized peace establishment

(a) It is the intent of Congress to provide an Army that is capable, in conjunction with the other armed forces, of

> **(1)** preserving the peace and security, and providing for the defense, of the United States, the Territories, Commonwealths, and possessions, and any areas occupied by the United States;
> **(2)** supporting the national policies;
> **(3)** implementing the national objectives; and
> **(4)** overcoming any nations responsible for aggressive acts that imperil the peace and security of the United States.

(b) In general, the Army, within the Department of the Army, includes land combat and service forces and such aviation and water transport as may be organic therein. It shall be organized, trained, and equipped primarily for prompt and sustained combat incident to operations on land. It is responsible for the preparation of land forces necessary for the effective prosecution of war except as otherwise assigned and, in accordance with integrated joint mobilization plans, for the expansion of the peacetime components of the Army to meet the needs of war.

(c) The Army consists of

> **(1)** the Regular Army, the Army National Guard of the United States, the Army National Guard while in the service of the United States and the Army Reserve; and
> **(2)** all persons appointed or enlisted in, or conscripted into, the Army without component.

(d) The organized peace establishment of the Army consists of all

> **(1)** military organizations of the Army with their installations and supporting and auxiliary elements, including combat, training, administrative, and logistic elements; and
> **(2)** members of the Army, including those not assigned to units; necessary to form the basis for a complete and immediate mobilization for the national defense in the event of a national emergency.

The United States Navy

TITLE 10, Subtitle C, PART I, CHAPTER 507.

Sec. 5062. United States Navy: composition; functions

(a) The Navy, within the Department of the Navy, includes, in general, naval combat and service forces and such aviation as may be organic therein. The Navy shall be organized, trained, and equipped primarily for prompt and sustained combat incident to operations at sea. It is responsible for the preparation of naval forces necessary for the effective prosecution of war except as otherwise assigned and, in accordance with integrated joint mobilization plans, for the expansion of the peacetime components of the Navy to meet the needs of war.

(b) All naval aviation shall be integrated with the naval service as part thereof within the Department of the Navy. Naval aviation consists of combat and service and training forces, and includes land-based naval aviation, air transport essential for naval operations, all air weapons and air techniques involved in the operations and activities of the Navy, and the entire remainder of the aeronautical organization of the Navy, together with the personnel necessary therefor.

(c) The Navy shall develop aircraft, weapons, tactics, technique, organization, and equipment of naval combat and service elements. Matters of joint concern as to these functions shall be coordinated between the Army, the Air Force, and the Navy

The United States Marine Corps

TITLE 10, Subtitle C, PART I, CHAPTER 507.

Sec. 5063. United States Marine Corps: composition; functions

(a) The Marine Corps, within the Department of the Navy, shall be so organized as to include not less than three combat divisions and three air wings, and such other land combat, aviation, and other services as may be organic therein. The Marine Corps shall be organized, trained, and equipped to provide fleet marine forces of combined arms, together with supporting air components, for service with the fleet in the seizure or defense of advanced naval bases and for the conduct of such land operations as may be essential to the prosecution of a naval campaign. In addition, the Marine Corps shall provide detachments and organizations for service on armed vessels of the Navy, shall provide security detachments for the protection of naval property at naval stations and bases, and shall perform such other duties as the President may direct. However, these additional duties may not detract from or interfere with the operations for which the Marine Corps is primarily organized.

(b) The Marine Corps shall develop, in coordination with the Army and the Air Force, those phases of amphibious operations that pertain to the tactics, technique, and equipment used by landing forces.

(c) The Marine Corps is responsible, in accordance with integrated joint mobilization plans, for the expansion of peacetime components of the Marine Corps to meet the needs of war

The United States Coast Guard

TITLE 14, PART I, CHAPTER 1.

Sec. 1. Establishment of Coast Guard

The Coast Guard as established January 28, 1915, shall be a military service and a branch of the armed forces of the United States at all times. The Coast Guard shall be a service in the Department of Homeland Security, except when operating as a service in the Navy

Sec. 2. Primary duties

The Coast Guard shall enforce or assist in the enforcement of all applicable Federal laws on, under, and over the high seas and waters subject to the jurisdiction of the United States; shall engage in maritime air surveillance or interdiction to enforce or assist in the enforcement of the laws of the United States; shall administer laws and promulgate and enforce regulations for the promotion of safety of life and property on and under the high seas and waters subject to the jurisdiction of the United States covering all matters not specifically delegated by law to some other executive department; shall develop, establish, maintain, and operate, with due regard to the requirements of national defense, aids to maritime navigation, ice-breaking facilities, and rescue facilities for the promotion of safety on, under, and over the high seas and waters subject to the jurisdiction of the United States; shall, pursuant to international agreements, develop, establish, maintain, and operate icebreaking facilities on, under, and over waters other than the high seas and waters subject to the jurisdiction of the United States; shall engage in oceanographic research of the high seas and in waters subject to the jurisdiction of the United States; and shall maintain a state of readiness to function as a specialized service in the Navy in time of war, including the fulfillment of Maritime Defense Zone command responsibilities.

APPENDIX 3

SERVICE VALUES

Service Values of the Armed Forces

AIR FORCE	ARMY	NAVY & MARINE CORPS
Integrity First	**Loyalty**	**Honor**
	Duty	
Service Before Self	**Respect**	**Courage**
	Selfless Service	
Excellence in All We Do	**Honor**	**Commitment**
	Integrity	
	Personal Courage	

COAST GUARD

Honor

Respect

Devotion to Duty

APPENDIX 4

CODE OF CONDUCT FOR MEMBERS OF THE UNITED STATES ARMED FORCES

I

I am an American, fighting in the forces which guard my country and our way of life. I am prepared to give my life in their defense.

II

I will never surrender of my own free will. If in command, I will never surrender the members of my command while they still have the means to resist.

III

If I am captured I will continue to resist by all means available. I will make every effort to escape and aid others to escape. I will accept neither parole nor special favors from the enemy.

IV

If I become a prisoner of war, I will keep faith with my fellow prisoners. I will give no information or take part in any action which might be harmful to my comrades. If I am senior, I will take command. If not, I will obey the lawful orders of those appointed over me and will back them up in every way.

V

When questioned, should I become a prisoner of war, I am required to give name, rank, service number and date of birth. I will evade answering further questions to the utmost of my ability. I will make no oral or written statements disloyal to my country and its allies or harmful to their cause.

VI

I will never forget that I am an American, fighting for freedom, responsible for my actions, and dedicated to the principles which made my country free. I will trust in my God and in the United States of America.

Executive Order 10631 (1955) as amended by EO 11382 (1967) and EO 12633 (1988)

APPENDIX 5

KEEPING YOUR HOUSE IN ORDER

Officers are expected to live balanced lives. They are expected to keep their professional and personal affairs, "their house," in order, to practice self-discipline on and off-duty, and to treat all moral, legal, and financial obligations responsibly. Officers anticipate deployment or periods of temporary duty with little or no advance notice. They must keep their financial and legal affairs current at all times, anticipating they may be called away for extended periods with very little time to tie up loose ends. Because military service places many restrictions on the freedom of movement, domicile, and conduct of all service members, officers assume a degree of responsibility for the welfare of their subordinates that is not typical of civilian managers. Officers are not only responsible that their houses are in order, but they must ensure that those of their subordinates are taken care of as well. Congress has enshrined this responsibility in the sections of Title 10, U.S. Code that create the service departments:

> All commanding officers and others in authority in the [Army, Naval Service, Air Force] are required … to take all necessary and proper measures, under the laws, regulations and customs of the [Army, Naval Service, Air Force], to promote and safeguard the morale, the physical well being, and the general welfare of the officers and enlisted persons under their command and charge.[1]

With that said, it is necessary to be clear about what officers owe their troops and crews. It honors your subordinates to remember they are Soldiers, Sailors, Marines, Coast Guardsmen, and Airmen; they are not your children or minor dependents. They are women and men who have voluntarily accepted the risks and necessary hardship that military service entails. All service members must accept primary responsibility for the character of their personal affairs, while their leaders must stand ready to provide general oversight, advice, counsel, and assistance.

This chapter describes keeping your house in order under the heads of personal responsibility, property accountability, and the balanced life.

Personal Responsibility

Officers are on duty 24 hours a day, seven days a week. They are responsible for living a respectable public life and their private affairs must be such that should they become known, they meet the standards of moral and ethical rectitude demanded by the public and the standards of the profession. Any private act that casts doubt on an officer's integrity, judgment, and reliability is grounds for negative evaluation of his or her career potential and, if serious enough, separation. Officers in sensitive situations will almost always lose the opportunity to perform the duties with which they are entrusted when other actions reflect badly on their judgment or reliability. Officers must be temperate in their use of alcohol, avoid overtly sexual public conduct and situations, especially in the presence of subordinates, and abstain entirely from illegal drugs. There is no faster way to terminate an officer's career than driving under the influence or showing up positive on a drug urinalysis.

It is particularly important for new officers to maintain financial stability. It goes without saying that officers are responsible for providing for the welfare of their dependents. They are also expected to settle all their just debts without fail. Most new officers have a daunting array of routine indebtedness: education loans, car payments, operating expenses, uniforms, and expenses related to setting up housekeeping. There are other routine expenses such as rent, utilities, eating, laundry and dry cleaning, and maintaining your appearance. The armed forces have a confusing and archaic pay system. Members draw different salaries depending on location, specialty, status, whether they are provided government quarters or live on the local economy, whether they are deployed or at home station, whether they receive rations in-kind, or buy their own. It is essential that they understand their eligibility for the various allowances that flesh out the monthly paycheck and actively manage their credit and indebtedness so it does not become a matter requiring intervention of the chain of command to protect the reputation of the service.

It is important when establishing eligibility for an allowance that the officers understand the circumstances under which eligibility for allowances ends. Many supplementary payments require presentation of receipts, so officers must develop habits of requesting and keeping records of expenditure required in performance of duty. Receipts documenting most expenses other than rations must accompany claims for reimbursement for travel and temporary duty, and there are a host of restrictions governing routine temporary duty arrangements, particularly acceptable lodging arrangements, about which service members should check with their local travel and finance offices prior to undertaking any obligation for payment that may turn out to be nonreimbursable. It is a fact that while all services are governed by the same Joint Travel Regulations (JTRs), services and local authorities often interpret the requirements of the JTRs differently.

The ease of establishing credit card accounts and running up excessive short-term indebtedness at a high interest rate is a genuine threat to new officers, new families, and enlisted subordinates. Officers must become experts on the Military Pay system, both to manage their own affairs and those of their subordinates. In addition, as a matter of personal survival, officers must practice self-discipline in managing their debt. It is essential to have a budget—one that provides for systematic savings against the likelihood of a rainy day.

Life insurance is required to provide for family members in case of the member's loss of life. Some kinds of life insurance can serve both as a form of savings and provide an immediate estate in event of death. Even single officers should be aware that most life insurance policies are much less expensive when acquired early in a career. The government underwritten Serviceman's Group Life Insurance (SGLI) provides a good foundation for a balanced insurance and savings program. Generally, service members will want to create a combination of immediately available savings, life insurance, and investment to prepare for their retirement, as well as provide for unanticipated financial requirements and provide for their families.

Besides managing their finances responsibly on a day-to-day basis, officers and all military members must remain mobile. An essential feature of mobility is ensuring rental contracts have a military clause that permits termination on short notice in the event of receipt of orders. Because most military personnel are paid by electronic deposit to a financial institution of their choice, all officers must establish an account to receive deposits. It is convenient to set this up for longer durations, rather than a single assignment, with an institution that caters to military members and is familiar with the mobile life style. Married officers must ensure continuity of support to dependent family members. Consideration should be given to opening a joint bank account. Nevertheless, dependent spouses should know what arrangements are in place prior to a member's deployment.

Commissioned leaders are responsible for ensuring that their subordinates have robust plans for the welfare of their families should the service member(s) be deployed on short notice. Single parents and married service couples are required to have family care plans that provide for the safekeeping of children in case of deployment. Officers must ensure their subordinates' plans are up to date and if they fall into one or the other of these categories that their own arrangements are current, foolproof, and that they have a plan B. Military families tend to live on-base or in communities close to home bases. It is traditional for military communities to take care of their own, particularly during periods of deployment.

Each service's traditions and standards are unique and have grown up to meet their particular rhythm of absences. Suffice to say, commanders at all levels realize that confidence in the welfare of family members during absence is an element of combat power. Officers have a positive responsibility to ensure their own subordinates anticipate the needs of their families during absences and that family networks exist to help those who suffer loss or unexpected emergencies while the service member is absent.

Officers should have a will. Personal property insurance is useful, particularly to cover losses of high-priced property like computers and other electronics. Officers with dependents may want to consider supplemental insurance to offset medical expenses for family care not covered by TRICARE, the Department of Defense-managed health care system.

Officers should build a personal file of copies of all important official documents and orders and keep it up to date. A current inventory of household goods is also useful. Most officers should have powers of attorney that permit someone to act in their stead if they are deployed without notice. Apartments have to be secured or closed (a housing allowance usually stops upon deployment for single service members), cars secured, bills paid, and so on. Marital status alone does not automatically entitle a spouse to act in the member's name. Because powers of attorney sign over great authority over one's affairs to another, they should not be entered into without legal advice from the Staff Judge Advocate Office. As a general rule, powers of attorney should be limited to performance of specific functions limiting the amount of harm that can be done if the trusted agent makes a mistake or breaks the trust implied in the instrument.

Property Accountability

There are few pitfalls that more often ensnare new officers than the responsibility to maintain accountability of government property in their care. Each service has its own regulations governing the detail of how accountability is to be maintained, however, in all services, the failure to maintain accountability and care for government property can lead to heavy personal financial liability—even where the property is not in the responsible party's immediate care. Some general rules are worth recounting.

First of all, officers must know what property they are accountable for. Ordinarily this is documented at unit level. However, many tool sets have separate components, identification of which requires reference to other sources or technical documents. Normally a unit supply officer or noncommissioned officer can identify the proper documents and listings.

Commanders are responsible for all the property assigned to their unit. They meet this responsibility by seeing to it that a chain of accountability is established from themselves to those who use the equipment to perform their duties. Where commanders fail to establish such formal accountability, they generally retain personal accountability as a matter of command. Even when the commander or subordinate leader has established user accountability by tying a particular user to a piece of equipment, the leader is responsible for ensuring that the property is maintained and present. Ordinarily the leader does this through a regular and systematic program of routine inspections and accountability inventories. Where equipment is found to be missing or damaged, the responsible commander takes appropriate action to replace or restore it and to establish financial liability for the loss to the government. For complex military equipment, loss or careless or wanton damage can lead to huge financial liabilities. Officers must know their responsibilities for property accountability and carry them out as a matter of the highest priority.

Balanced Life

Finally, officers are expected to live balanced lives and do everything they can to see that their subordinates have the opportunity to do the same. Balanced lives involve the care in proportion of the physical, material, mental, and spiritual well being of each service member and of their family members. Physical well being involves both the maintenance of the service member's physical condition and the provision of required medical care for members and their families. TRICARE is a regionally managed health care program for active duty and retired members of the military services, their families, and survivors. All active duty members are automatically enrolled in TRICARE and, for the most part, receive medical care at no cost through military medical facilities. Family members must be enrolled in one of a number of TRICARE programs, each differentiated by available services, provider choice, and out-of-pocket costs. Family members are not eligible for uniformed dental care, but supplemental insurance programs for dependent dental care are available at a minimal cost. Because TRICARE is a complex program, service members with families will want to inform themselves fully of the details of available covered services and services requiring out-of-pocket expense before selecting the particular program suitable for their needs.

Material well being for service members has to do with access to the best equipment available to accomplish their mission. Officers have a number of roles ensuring their subordinates receive and maintain the government equipment necessary for their mission. For family members, it has to do with the presence of shelter, food, and safety to members living in organized military communities. While the provision of these resources is beyond the purview of most officers, they do have the obligation to ensure that they and their subordinates are aware of the resources available to them and have access to them in accordance with existing service regulations. Officers also become involved when subordinates fail to maintain adequately the resources provided.

In addition to salary, service members receive housing or a housing allowance as part of their payment for service. Because the Department of Defense is engaged in the long-term process of outsourcing military housing, a number of different programs exist for management of housing resources. Where government housing is available, members can be required to live on-post to maintain facility usage or, where housing is scarce, they may have to live off-base and wait a long time before government housing becomes available. Where housing is not available on a military installation, a base housing office will normally assist members locating approved housing with costs commensurate with the available housing allowance. When on detached service, it is the member's responsibility to know what the housing allowance will cover before overextending himself or herself on housing costs. Again, a military clause in all rental contracts is essential. When living off-base, it is always wise to inquire about monthly utility costs and to anticipate requirements for initial deposits equal to a month's rent and utility costs. Housing allowances are supplemented in high-cost areas, but it cannot be assumed that the allowance and supplement will be fully adequate to fund the off-base housing the member finds desirable.

Mental and spiritual needs are provided for by allowing members time off from the press of duty and encouraging and supporting their spiritual, professional, and intellectual development. All officers must take time off from their day-to-day concerns to refresh their batteries and reorient their thinking. There is little more important that an officer can do to help his subordinates balance their lives than to make their off-duty time reasonably predictable, while ensuring a command climate that encourages their personal development and well being, and one that guarantees family members will be properly cared for in their absences. Officers must continue to grow professionally and intellectually. They must plan for and take every opportunity to enhance their professional and civil education and encourage and support their subordinates to do the same.

Military service, with its shared dangers, hardships, and periods of separation from family and loved ones, produces both great personal stress within individual service members and strong bonds of attachment within units. Uncertainty, chaos, and fear pervade the battle space. Experience shows that forces whose members can best control their fear and channel it into cohesive action usually win the battle. Human losses are a regular part of battle, thus the requirement for military men's and women's spiritual comfort in the face of loss, to make sense of the irrational and horrific, is a part of providing for both member and unit well being. Those who face death together share a bond unique in human society. Grieving is a part of the collective esprit of any combat organization, just as it is for first-responders at home. The welfare of the service member's spirit, unique to each of them and their particular view of the world and life, is fostered too by membership in a unique culture with its own sense of moral community and feeling of accomplishment in service and sacrifice to a higher purpose—the preservation of the republic and its way of life. The shared uniforms, ceremonies, traditions, and values of our military services all reinforce the spiritual kinship of their members as a people set apart, performing an essential service for the wider society.

Even in peacetime, prolonged separation and concern for distant family members places heavy emotional stress on young Soldiers, Sailors, Airmen, Coast Guardsmen, and Marines. Many military members define themselves and their view of the world and life according to a faith-based religion and find emotional strength in religious observation and ceremony. Others find their view of reality in nature, philosophy, or other human beings. Regardless of one's world view, as officers of a secular republic with a constitution mandating religious neutrality, the leader must walk a careful line. He or she must be sensitive to the needs of all their subordinates, irrespective of their world views, ensuring access to whatever ministrations they find of spiritual comfort without promoting or denigrating any or none. The same comfort and pride must be extended to member's families who bear their own burdens in most cases without the strength drawn from direct membership and acknowledged participation. Family support groups, access to religious and other spiritual support, and public observations of respect and appreciation for the sacrifice of those lost or injured are an important part of military life.

Members of today's armed forces are largely married, sometimes to fellow service members. Married service members particularly feel the strain of balancing personal and professional responsibilities that are not diminished just because of parenthood. The services are demanding masters, expecting that duty for all members will take priority over the convenience and sometimes even the welfare of the family. Service families are expected to be largely self-reliant. The services provide a variety of community support agencies, often sustained largely by volunteer labor of family members that can help service members and their families deal with the vicissitudes of service life. Officers as leaders must know what these services are, encourage their support, and know how to gain access to them for their subordinates. It is a truism that services develop Soldiers, Sailors, Airmen, Marines, and Coastguardsmen and reenlist families. However, families are expected to do their part to sustain their quality of community life.

APPENDIX 6

"THE MEANING OF YOUR COMMISSION"
FROM THE 1950 EDITION OF *THE ARMED FORCES OFFICER*

Upon being commissioned in the Armed Services of the United States, a man incurs a lasting obligation to cherish and protect his country and to develop within himself that capacity and reserve strength which will enable him to serve its arms and the welfare of his fellow Americans with increasing wisdom, diligence and patriotic conviction.

This is the meaning of his commission. It is not modified by any reason of assignment while in the service, nor is the obligation lessened in the day an officer puts the uniform aside and returns to civil life. Having been specially chosen by the United States to sustain the dignity and integrity of its sovereign power, an officer is expected so to maintain himself and so to exert his influence for so long as he may live, that he will be recognized as a worthy symbol of all that is best in the national character.

In this sense the trust imposed in the highest military commander in the land is not more than what is encharged the newest ensign or second lieutenant. Nor is it less. It is the fact of commission which gives special distinction to the man and in turn requires that the measure of his devotion to the service of his country be distinctive, as compared with the charges laid upon the average citizen.

In the beginning, a man takes an oath to uphold his country's Constitution against all enemies foreign and domestic, to bear true faith and allegiance, and to discharge well and faithfully the duties of office.He does this without any mental reservation.

Thereafter he is given a paper which says that because the President as a representative of the people of this country reposes "special trust and confidence" in his patriotism, valor, fidelity, and abilities," he is forthwith commissioned.

By these tokens, the Nation also becomes a party to the contract, and will faithfully keep its bond with the man. While he continues to serve honorably, it will sustain him and will clothe him with its dignity. That it has vouched for him gives him a felicitous status in our society. The device he wears, his insignia, and

149

even his garments identify him directly with the power of the United States. The living standards of himself and of his family are underwritten by Federal statue. Should he become ill, the Nation will care for him. Should he be disabled, it will stand as his guardian through life. Should he seek to advance himself through higher studies, it will open the way.

Other than the officer corps, there is no group within our society toward which the obligation of the Nation is more fully expressed. Even so, other Americans regard this fact with pride, rather that with envy. They accept the principle that some unusual advantage should attend exceptional and unremitting responsibility. Whatever path an American officer may walk, he enjoys prestige. Though little is known of his intrinsic merit, he will be given the respect of his fellow citizens, unless he proves himself utterly undeserving.

The national esteem for the corps is one of the priceless assets of American society. The services themselves so recognize it. That the place such strong emphasis upon the importance of personal honor among officers is because they know that the future of our arms and the well-being of our people depend upon a constant renewing and strengthening of public faith in the virtue of the corps. Were this to languish, the Nation would be loath to commit its sons to any military endeavor, no matter how grave the emergency.

The works of goodwill by which those who lead the national military forces endeavor to win the undeserved trust of the American people is one of the chief preservatives of the American people is one of the American system of freedoms. The character of the corps is in a most direct sense of final safeguard of the character of the Nation.

To these thoughts any officer who is morally deserving of his commission would freely subscribe. He will look beyond the letter of his obligation and will accept in his own heart the total implications of his new responsibility.

So doing, he still might see fit to ask: "But to what do I turn my thoughts? How do I hold myself so that while following the line of duty, I will also exemplify those ideas which may inspire other men to make their best effort?"

It is suggested that there is a one-word key to answer among four lofty qualities which are cited on every man's commission.

That word is Fidelity.

As for patriotism, either a man loves his country or else he would not seek commission at its hands, unless he be completely the rascal, pretending to serve in order to destroy.

Valor, on the other hand, can not be fully vouchsafed, since it is not given to any man to know the nature and depth of his personal courage.

Abilities vary from man to man, and are partly what heredity and environment have made them. If nature had not imposed a ceiling, mere striving would make every man a genius.

But fidelity is the derivative of personal decision. It is the jewel within reach of every man who has the will to possess it.

Given an officer corps composed throughout of men who would make the eternal try toward bettering their professional capabilities and furthering the working efficiency and harmony within all forces, the United States would become thrice armed though not producing one new weapon in its arsenals.

Great faith, rightness of mind, influence over other men, and finally, personal success and satisfaction come of service to the ideals of the profession. Were these strengths reflected throughout the officer body, it could well happen that because of the shining example, the American people would become more deeply conscious of the need to keep their own fibers strong than has been their disposition throughout history.

Accepting these truths as valid, a man still must know where he stands before making a true reckoning of his line of advance. This entails some consideration of himself (a) as to the personal standard which is required if him because of his position in relation to all others (b) as to the reason in common sense which make this requirement, and (c) as to the principles and philosophy which will enable him to play his part well.

The military officer is considered a gentleman, not because Congress wills it, nor because it has been the custom of people in all times to afford him that courtesy, but specifically because nothing less than a gentleman is truly suited for his particular set of responsibilities.

This is not simply a bit of self-adulation; it is distinctly the American tradition in the matter. The Nation has never attempted to draw its officers from a particular class. During World War II, thousands if men were commissioned in our forces who enjoyed little opportunity in their earlier environments. They were sound by nature. They had courage. They could set a good example. They could rally other men around them. In the eyes of the services, these things count more that any man's blood lines. We say with Voltaire, "Whoever serves his country well has no need of ancestors."

On the other hand, from the time of the Colonies, this country has despised press gangs, flogging, martinetism, and all of the other Old World military practices which demanded the rank and file. Its military system was founded on the dignity of man, just as was its Constitution. The system has sought ever since to advance itself by appealing to the higher nature of the individual. That is why its officers need to be gentlemen. To call forth great loyalty in other people and to harness it to any noble undertaking, one must first be sensible of their fines instincts and feelings. Certainly these things at least are among the gentle qualities which are desired in every military officer of the United States:

1. Strong belief in human rights.
2. Respect for the dignity of every other person.

3. The Golden Rule attitude toward one's daily associates.
4. An abiding interest in all aspects of human welfare.
5. A willingness to deal with every man as considerately as if he were a blood relative.

These qualities are the epitome of strength, not of softness.

They mark the man who is capable of pursuing the great purpose consistently in spite of temptations. He who possesses them will all the more surely be regarded as a "man among men." Take any crowd of new recruits! The greater number of them during their first few days in service will use more profanity and obscenity, talk more about women and boast more about drinking than they have ever done in their lives, because of the mistaken idea that this is the quick way to get a reputation for being hard-boiled. But at the same time, the one or two men among them who stay decent, talk moderately and walk the line of duty will uniquely receive the infinite respect of the others. It never fails to happen!

There is the other matter about how a man should feel toward his own profession. Simply to accept the fact that the bearing of arms is a highly honorable calling because the book says so should not suffice one's own interest in the matter, when a little personal reflection will reveal wherein the honor resides.

To every officer who has thought earnestly about the business, it is at once apparent that civilization, as men have known it since the time of the Greek City States, has rested as a pyramid upon a base if organized military power. Moreover, the general possibility of world culture progress in the foreseeable future has no other conceivable foundation. For any military man to deny, on any ground whatever, the role which his profession has played in the establishment of everything which is well-ordered in our society, shows only a faulty understanding of history. It made possible the birth of the American system of freedoms. Later, it gave the nation a new birth and vouchsafed a more perfect union.

Likewise, we need to see the case in its present terms. One may abhor war fully, despise militarism absolutely, deplore all o the impulses in human nature which make armed force necessary, and still agree that for t he world as we know it, the main hope is that "peace-loving nations can be made obviously capable of defeating nations which are willing to wage aggressive war." Those words, by the way were not said by a warrior, but by the eminent pacifists, Bertrand Russell. It does not make the military man any less the humanitarian that he accepts this reality, that he faces toward the chance forth-rightly, and that he believes that id all military power were stricken tomorrow, men would revert to a state of anarchy and there would ensue the total defeat of the forces which are trying to establish peace and brotherly love in our lives.

The complete identity of American military force with the character of the people comes of this indivisibility of interest. To think of the military as a guardian class apart, like Lynches "born for vision, ordained for watching" rather than as a strong right arm, corporately joined to the body and sharing its every function, is historically false and politically inaccurate. It is not unusual, however, for those whose task it is to interpret the trend of opinion to take the line that "the military" are thinking one way and "the people" quite another on some particular issue, as if to imply that the two are quite separate and of different nature. This is usually false in detail, and always false in general. It not only discounts the objects of their unity but overlooks the truth of its origins.

Maybe they should be invited to go to the root of the word. The true meaning of "populous," from which we get the word "people," was in the time of ancient Rome the "armed body." The pure-blooded Roman in the days of the Republic could not conceive of a citizen who was not a warrior. It was the arms which Roman's possession of land enabled him to get that qualified him to participate in the affairs of state. He had no political rights until he had fought. He was not of the people; they were of him.

Nor is this concept alien to the ideals on which Founding Fathers built the American system, since they stated it as the right and duty of every able-bodied citizen to bear arms.

These propositions should mean much to every American who has chosen the military profession. A main point is that on becoming an officer a man does not renounce any part of his fundamental character as an American citizen. He has simply signed on for the post graduate course where one learns hoe to exercise authority un accordance with the spirit of liberty. The nature of his trusteeship has been subtly expressed by an Admiral in our service: "The American philosophy places the individual above the state. It distrusts personal power and coercion. It denies the existence of indispensable men. It asserts the supremacy of principle."

An understanding of American principles of life and growth, and personal zeal in upholding them, is the bedrock of sound leading in our services. Moral and emotional stability are expected of an American officer; he can usually satisfy his superiors if he attains to this equilibrium. But he is not likely to satisfy himself unless he can also achieve that maturity of character which expresses itself in the ability to make decisions in the detachment of spirit from that which is pleasant or unpleasant to him personally, in the desire to hold onto things not by grasping them but by understanding them and remembering them, and in learning to covet only that which may be rightfully possessed.

An occasional man has become wealthy while in the services by making wise investments, through writings by skills at invention, or through some other means. But he is the exception. The majorities have no such prospect. Indeed, if love of money were the mainspring of all American actions, the officer corps long since would have disintegrated. But it is well said that the only truly happy people on earth are those who are indifferent to money because they have some positive purpose which forecloses it. Than the service, there is no other environment which is more conductive to the leading of the full life by the individual who is ready to accept the word of the philosopher that the only security on earth is the willingness to accept insecurity as an inevitable part of living. Once an officer has made this passage into maturity, and is at peace with himself because the service means more to him than all else, he will find kinship with the great body of his brothers-in-arms. The highest possible consequences can develop from the feelings of men mutually inspired by some great endeavor and moving forward together according to the principle that only those who are willing to serve are fit to lead. Completely immersed in action they have no time for smallness in speech, thought or deed. It is for these reasons that those who in times past have excelled in the leadership of American forces have invariably been great Americans first and superior offers second. The rule applies at all levels. The lieutenant who is not moved at the thought that he is serving his country is unlikely to do an intelligent job of directing other men. He will come apart at the seams whenever the going grows tough. Until men accept this thought freely, and apply it to their personal action, it is not possible for them to go forward together strongly. In the words of Lionel Curtis: "The only force that unites men is conscience, a varying capacity in most of them to put the interests of other people before their own."

The services are accustomed to being hammered. Like other human institutions, they are imperfect. Therefore the criticisms are not always unjust. Further, there is no more reason why the services should be immune to attack than any other organic part of our society and government.

The service officer is charged only to take a lively interest in all such discussions. He has no more right to condemn the service unfairly then has any other American. On the other hand he is not expected to be an intellectual eunuch, oblivious to all of the faults in the institution to which he gives his loyalty. To the contrary, the nature of that loyalty requires that he will use his force toward the righting of those things which reason convinces him are going wrong, though making certain that his action will not do more damage than repair.

His ultimate commanding loyalty at all times is to his country, and not to his service or his superior. He owes it to his country to speak the truth as he sees it. This implies a steadying judgment as to when it should be spoken, and to whom it should be addressed. A truth need not only be well-rounded, but the utterance of it should be cognizant of the stresses and objectives of the hour. Truth becomes falsehood unless it has the strength of perspective. The presentation of facts is self-justifying only when the facts are developed in their true proportion.

Where there is public criticism of the services, in matters both large and small, the service officer has the right and the duty of intervention only toward the end of making possible that all criticism will be well-informed. That right can not be properly exercised when there is nothing behind it but a defense of professional pride. The duty can be well performed when the officer knows not only his subject —the mechanism itself—but the history and philosophy of the armed services in their relation to the development of the American system. Criticism from the outside is essential to service well-being, for as Confucius said, oftentimes men in the game are blind to what the lookers on see clearly.

The value of any officer's opinion of any military question can never be any greater than the extent and accuracy of his information. His ability to dispose public though favorably toward the service will depend upon the wisdom of his words rather than upon his military rank and other credentials. A false idea will come upon a bad fate even though it has the backing of the highest authority.

Only men of informed mind and unprejudiced expression can strengthen the claim of the services on the affections of the American people.

This is, of itself, a major objective for the officer corps, since our public has little studious interest in military affairs, tends ever to discount the vitality of the military role in the progress and prosperity of the nation and regards the security problem as one of the less pleasant and abnormal burdens on an otherwise orderly existence.

It is an explicable contradiction of the American birthright that to some of our people the military establishment is at best a necessary evil, and military service is an extraordinary hardship rather than an inherent obligation. Yet these illusions are rooted deep in the American tradition, though it is a fact to be noted not without hope that we are growing wiser as we move along. In the years which followed the American Revolution, the new union of States tried to eliminate military forces altogether. There was vast confusion of thought as to what freedom required for its own survival. Thomas Jefferson, one of the great architects of democracy, an still renowned for his "isolationist" sentiments, wrote the warning: "We must train and classify the whole of our male citizens, and make military instruction a regular part of collegiate education. We can never be safe until this is done."

None the less, the hour came when the standing Army was reduced to 80 men. None the less, the quaint notion has survived that an enlightened interest in military affairs is somehow undemocratic. And none the less, recurring war has invariably found the United States inadequately prepared for the defense of its own territory.

Because there has been a hold-over of these mistaken sentiments right down to the present, there persists in many military officers a defensive attitude toward their own profession, which has no practical relation to the strength of the ground on which they are enabled to stand. Toward any unfair and flippant criticism of the "military mind" they react with resentment, instead of with buoyant proof that their own minds are more plastic and more receptive to national ideals than those of any other profession. Where they should approach all problems of the national security with the zeal of the missionary, seeking and giving light, they treat this subject as if it were a private game preserve.

It suffices to say of this minority that they are a barnacle on the hull of an otherwise staunch vessel. From such limited concepts of personal responsibility, there can not fail to develop a foreshortened view of the dignity of the task at hand. The note of apology is injected at the wrong time; the tone of belligerency is used when it serves no purpose. When someone arises within the halls of government to say that the military establishment of "uneconomic" because it cuts no bricks, bales no hay and is not unusual to hear some military men concur in this strange notion. That acquiescence is wholly unbecoming.

The physician is not slurred as belonging to a nonproductive profession because he contributes only to the care and healing of the body, and though these things to the general well-being of society. Respect for formal education, organized religion and all of the enterprises built up around the dissemination of ideas is not the less because the resultant benefit to society is not always tangible and saleable. Hence to say that that without which society could not endure in its present form is "uneconomic" is to make the word itself altogether meaningless.

In that inner power of courage and conviction, which stems from the spiritual integrity of the individual, lies the strength of democracy. As to their ability to produce toward these ends, the military services can stand on the record. When shortly after World War II, a census was taken among the returned men, 60 percent said that they had been morally strengthened by their military service in the American uniform. About 30 percent had no opinion or felt that military life had not changed them one way or the other. An insignificant minority considered themselves damaged. This is an amazing testimony in light of the fact that only a small fraction of American youth is schooled to believe that any spiritual good can come of military service. As to what it signifies, those who take a wholly materialistic view of the objects of the Republic are entitled to call the military establishment "uneconomic." The services will continue to hold with the idea that strong nationhood comes not of the making of gadgets but of the building of character.

Men beget goodwill in other men by giving it. They develop courage in their following mainly as a reflection of the courage which they show in their own action. These two qualities of mind and heart are of the essence of sound officership. One is of little avail without the other, and either helps to sustain the other. As to which is the stronger force in its impact upon the masses of men, no truth is more certain than the words once written by William James:

> Evident though the shortcomings of a man may be, if he is ready to give up
> his life for a cause, we forgive him everything. However inferior he may be

to ourselves in other respects, if we cling to life while he throws it away like a flower, we bow to his superiority.

Theodore Roosevelt once said that if he had a son who refrained from any worthwhile action because ot the fear of hurt to himself, he would disown him. Soon after his return to civilian life, General Dwight D. Eisenhower spoke of the worthwhileness of "living dangerously." An officer of the United States armed forces can not go far wrong if he holds with these ideas. It is not the suitable profession for those who believe only in digging-in and nursing a soft snap until death comes at a ripe old age. Who risks nothing gains nothing.

Nor should there be any room in it for professional smugness, small jealousies, and undue concern about privilege.

The regular recognizes as peer and comrade the officer from any of the civilian components. That he is a professional does not give him an especial eminence, but simply a greater measure of responsibility for the success of the total establishment. Moreover, he can not afford to be patronizing, without risking self-embarrassment, such is the vast experience which many reservists have had on the active field of war.

Toward services other than his own, any officer is expected to have both a comradely feeling and an imaginative interest. Any Army officer is a better man for having studied the works of Admiral Mahan and familiarized himself with the modern Navy from first-hand experience. Those who lead sea-going forces can enlarge their own capacities by knowing more, rather than less, about the nature of the air and ground establishments. The submariner can always learn something useful to his own work by mingling with airmen; the airman becomes a better officer as he grows in qualified knowledge of ground and sea fighting.

But the fact remains that the services are not alike, that no wit of man can make them alike, and that the retention by each of its separate character, customs and confidence is essential to the conserving of our national military power. Unification has not altered this basic proposition. The first requirement of a unified establishment is moral soundness in each of the integral parts, without which there can be no soundness at all. And on question of fundamental loyalty, the officer who loves every other service just as much as his own will have just as much active virtue as the man who loves other women as much as his wife.

FOUNDATIONS OF AN OFFICER'S LIBRARY

Arrian, *The Campaigns of Alexander*, trans. Aubrey de Selincourt (Penguin Books, 1971).

Christopher R. Browning, *Ordinary Men: Reserve Police Battalion 101 and the Final Solution in Poland* (Harper Perennial, 1993).

Caesar, *The Civil War*, trans. Jane F. Gardner (Penguin Books, 1967).

Carl von Clausewitz, *On War*, indexed edition, edited and translated by Michael Howard and Peter Paret (Princeton: Princeton University Press, 1984).

Stephen Covey, *7 Habits of Highly Effective People* (Simon & Schuster, 2005).

Martin van Creveld, *Supplying War: Logistics from Wallenstein to Patton* (Cambridge: Cambridge University Press, 1977).

Frederick Crews, Sandra Schor, and Michael Hennessy, *The Borzoi Handbook for Writers* (McGraw Hill, 1993).

C. S. Forester, E. H. Simmons, ed., *Rifleman Dodd* (Nautical and Aviation Publishing Company of America, 1990).

J. F. C. Fuller, *The Conduct of War: 1789–1961* (New Brunswick, NJ: Rutgers University Press, 1961).

Azar Gat, *A History of Military Thought: From the Enlightenment to the Cold War* (London: Oxford University Press, 2001).

Michael I. Handel. *Masters of War: Sun Tzu, Clausewitz and Jomini* (London: Frank Cass, 1992).

Victor Davis Hanson, *Carnage and Culture: Landmark Battles in the Rise of Western Power* (Doubleday, 2001).

Anthony E. Hartle, *Moral Issues in Military Decision Making* (Lawrence, KS: University Press of Kansas, 2004).

Homer, *The Iliad*, trans. Robert Fagles (Penguin Books, 1990).

Michael Eliot Howard, *War in European History* (Oxford: Oxford University Press, 1976).

Elbert Hubbard, *A Message to Garcia*, at http://www.birdsnest.com/garcia.htm.

Michael Ignatieff, *The Warrior's Honor* (Vintage, 1999).

Baron Antoine Henri de Jomini, *The Art of War* (Greenhill Books, 1996).

John Keegan. *The Face of Battle. A Study of Agincourt, Waterloo and the Somme* (London: Penguin Books, 1976).

Rushworth M. Kidder, *How Good People Make Tough Choices* (Fireside, 1996).

James M. McPherson. *Battle Cry of Freedom: The Civil War Era (Oxford History of the United States)* (Oxford: Oxford University Press, 2003).

Williamson Murray, MacGregor Knox and Alvin Bernstein, eds. *The Making of Strategy: Rulers, States, and War* (Cambridge: Cambridge University Press, 1994).

Williamson Murray and Allan R. Millett, eds., *Military Innovation in the Interwar Period* (Cambridge: Cambridge University Press, 1996).

Anton Myrer, *Once An Eagle* (New York: Harper Torch).

Peter Paret, Gordon Craig, and Felix Gilbert, eds., *Makers of Modern Strategy: from Machiavelli to the Nuclear Age* (Princeton, NJ: Princeton University Press, 1986).

Donald Phillips, *Lincoln on Leadership* (New York: Warner Books, 1992).

Donald T. Phillips and James M. Loy, *Character in Action: The U.S. Coast Guard on Leadership* (U.S. Naval Institute Press, 2003).

Colin Powell, *My American Journey* (New York: Random House, 1996).

Edgar Puryear, *American Generalship: Character is Everything: The Art of Command* (Novato, CA: Presidio Press).

Michael Shaara, *The Killer Angels* (New York: Ballantine Books, 1993).

John Shy, *A People Numerous & Armed* (Ann Arbor, MI: University of Michigan Press, 1990).

Eugene B. Sledge, *With the Old Breed: At Peleliu and Okinawa* (Oxford: Oxford University Press, reprint 1990).

Jim Stockdale, *Thoughts of a Philosophical Fighter Pilot* (Hoover Institution Press, 1995).

Robert B. Strassler, *The Landmark Thucydides: A Comprehensive Guide to the Peloponnesian War* (Simon & Schuster, 1996).

Harry G. Summers, Jr. *On Strategy: A Critical Analysis of the Vietnam War* (New York, NY: Dell Publishing, 1982).

Earnest Dunlop Swinton, *Defence of Duffer's Drift* (Avery Publishing Group, reprint edition, May 1, 1986).

Sun Tzu, *The Art of War*. trans. Samuel B. Griffith (Oxford: Oxford University Press, 1963).

Thucydides, *History of the Peloponnesian War*. trans. Rex Warner (New York and London: Penguin Books, 1954).

Michael Walzer, *Just and Unjust Wars*, Third Edition (New York: Basic Books, 2000).

Russell F. Weigley, *The Age of Battles: The Quest for Decisive Warfare from Brietenfeld to Waterloo* (Bloomington: Indiana University Press, 1991).

———. *Towards an American Army: Military Thought from Washington to Marshall* (Westport, CT: Greenwood Press, 1962).

ACKNOWLEDGMENTS

This book was written by a team of authors representing the superintendents of the Military, Naval, Air Force, and Coast Guard Academies, with participation and support of the Marine Corps University. The authors were serving and retired officers and civilian faculty members, both women and men. Because *The Armed Forces Officer* has traditionally been a Department of Defense publication, early sponsorship for the project was sought from the Joint Staff J-7. Congressman Ike Skelton, a longtime supporter of professional military education, agreed to provide a Foreword as did the Chairman, Joint Chiefs of Staff. The authors drafted the chapters individually and edited them collectively according to an organization, and with a concept of what it means to be an Armed Forces Officer, developed together at the beginning of the drafting process. The effort has been guided by the spirit of the United States of America: *E Pluribus Unum*. Contributing authors (their organizational affiliations when they worked on this project) were:

Colonel Michael F. Campbell, USMC, Deputy Director, Center for the Study of Professional Military Ethics, U.S. Naval Academy.

Captain Robert L. Desh, USCG, Director, Leadership Development Center, U.S. Coast Guard Academy.

Dr. John T. Farquhar, Lt Col, USAF, Ret., Associate Professor of Military Strategic Studies, U.S. Air Force Academy.

Dr. Jennifer Griffiths, Leadership Development Center, U.S. Coast Guard Academy.

Colonel Jon Hull, USMC, Marine Corps University.

Colonel Robyn M. King, PhD, USAF, U.S. Air Force Academy and Air University.

Major Daniel R. Moy, USAF, Assistant Professor Department of History, U.S. Air Force Academy.

Dr. Albert C. Pierce, Director, Center for the Study of Professional Military Ethics, U.S. Naval Academy.

Lieutenant Colonel Gary E. Slyman, USMC, Deputy Director, Center for the Study of Professional Military Ethics, U.S. Naval Academy.

Dr. Richard Swain, William E. Simon Center for the Professional Military Ethic, U.S. Military Academy.

Debbie Beck, Editor.

Layout and design by Joint Staff Support Services Office, Pentagon and second edition by Potomac Books, Inc.